EDUCATION IN A COMPETITIVE AND GLOBALIZING WORLD

SCIENCE TEACHING AND LEARNING

PRACTICES, IMPLEMENTATION AND CHALLENGES

EDUCATION IN A COMPETITIVE AND GLOBALIZING WORLD

Additional books and e-books in this series can be found on Nova's website under the Series tab.

EDUCATION IN A COMPETITIVE AND GLOBALIZING WORLD

SCIENCE TEACHING AND LEARNING

PRACTICES, IMPLEMENTATION AND CHALLENGES

PAUL J. HENDRICKS
EDITOR

Copyright © 2020 by Nova Science Publishers, Inc.

All rights reserved. No part of this book may be reproduced, stored in a retrieval system or transmitted in any form or by any means: electronic, electrostatic, magnetic, tape, mechanical photocopying, recording or otherwise without the written permission of the Publisher.

We have partnered with Copyright Clearance Center to make it easy for you to obtain permissions to reuse content from this publication. Simply navigate to this publication's page on Nova's website and locate the "Get Permission" button below the title description. This button is linked directly to the title's permission page on copyright.com. Alternatively, you can visit copyright.com and search by title, ISBN, or ISSN.

For further questions about using the service on copyright.com, please contact:
Copyright Clearance Center
Phone: +1-(978) 750-8400   Fax: +1-(978) 750-4470   E-mail: info@copyright.com.

NOTICE TO THE READER

The Publisher has taken reasonable care in the preparation of this book, but makes no expressed or implied warranty of any kind and assumes no responsibility for any errors or omissions. No liability is assumed for incidental or consequential damages in connection with or arising out of information contained in this book. The Publisher shall not be liable for any special, consequential, or exemplary damages resulting, in whole or in part, from the readers' use of, or reliance upon, this material. Any parts of this book based on government reports are so indicated and copyright is claimed for those parts to the extent applicable to compilations of such works.

Independent verification should be sought for any data, advice or recommendations contained in this book. In addition, no responsibility is assumed by the Publisher for any injury and/or damage to persons or property arising from any methods, products, instructions, ideas or otherwise contained in this publication.

This publication is designed to provide accurate and authoritative information with regard to the subject matter covered herein. It is sold with the clear understanding that the Publisher is not engaged in rendering legal or any other professional services. If legal or any other expert assistance is required, the services of a competent person should be sought. FROM A DECLARATION OF PARTICIPANTS JOINTLY ADOPTED BY A COMMITTEE OF THE AMERICAN BAR ASSOCIATION AND A COMMITTEE OF PUBLISHERS.

Additional color graphics may be available in the e-book version of this book.

Library of Congress Cataloging-in-Publication Data

ISBN: 978-1-53617-406-9

Published by Nova Science Publishers, Inc. † New York

CONTENTS

Preface   **vii**

Chapter 1   STEM Integration:
Evidences of Students' Learning   **1**
*Mónica Baptista, Iva Martins and
Teresa Conceição*

Chapter 2   Technology-Based Science Teaching among
Gifted Females in Singapore:
Attitudes and Learning Environment   **27**
G. Sundari Pramathevan and Barry J. Fraser

Chapter 3   The Problem of Perception:
Challenging Students' Views of Science and
Scientists through School-Scientist Partnerships   **67**
Garry Falloon

Chapter 4   The Effects of Discovery Learning Supported with
Learning Boxes on Students' Academic
Achievement, Competences for Learning Science
and Science Attitude   **111**
Hülya Aslan Efe, Nazan Bakir and Rifat Efe

Chapter 5	An Integrated NOS Map on Nature of Science Based on the Philosophy of Science, and the Dimensions of Learning in Science *Jun-Young Oh, Yeon-A Son and* *Norman G. Lederman*	**147**
Index		**169**

PREFACE

This compilation aims to analyse students' learning during STEM activities in the following categories: real-world problem solving and knowledge about the topic under discussion. This study is part of a larger project that comprises five school clusters and involves students from several grades.

Next, the authors develop, validate and apply an attitude and learning environment questionnaire for gifted female students to evaluate technology-based science instruction by comparing regular and technology-based science classrooms.

Additionally, Science Teaching and Learning: Practices, Implementation and Challenges reports the methods and outcomes of a study that explored the impact of a six-month school-scientist partnership involving a New Zealand science research institute and a group of 164 9-10 year olds.

The authors investigate the effects of learning boxes on 5th grade students' academic achievement and retention in science classes. In order to realize this goal, a quantitative research method including an experimental design was used.

The concluding study considers Kuhn's concept of how scientific revolution takes place based on individual elements or tenets of the nature of science, and explores the interrelationships within the individual elements or tenets of the nature of science.

Chapter 1 - This chapter aims to analyse the students' learning, during the development of STEM activities, in the following categories: real-world problem solving, knowledge about the topic under discussion and design. This study is part of a larger project that comprised five school clusters, involving students from several grades. In this chapter, the authors have chosen to focus in one of the school clusters and in two STEM activities (color of our houses and dye wool). These activities were performed by 119 students belonging to 3rd and 4th grade. Both activities were designed considering the five dimensions described by Thibaut et al. (2018) and were planned in alignment with the national curriculum for the elementary school. Results show that students indeed understood scientific concepts (i.e., knowledge about the topic under discussion), as well as developed scientific competences through solving problems related with their local context by inquiry-based learning. The results also showed that the activities allowed students to apply scientific knowledge in building house replicas and manufacturing wool accessories (i.e., design). Additionally, in order to well-succeed on these actions, students had to work with others, communicating and negotiating meanings and positions, and confronting in a respectful manner others' ideas and positions. These are all important competencies that are commonly agreed that citizens should have.

Chapter 2 - This science education study was the first in Singapore to focus on gifted female students in technology-based classrooms in a secondary-school setting. The authors developed, validated and used an attitude and learning environment questionnaire for gifted female students to evaluate technology-based science instruction by comparing regular and technology-based science classrooms. This questionnaire contains four attitude scales (Attitudes to Computers, Task Value, Self-efficacy and Self-regulation) and six learning environment scales (Investigation, Task Orientation, Collaboration, Differentiation, Computer Usage and Formative Assessment). For the authors' sample of 722 students (379 students in 14 technology-based science classrooms and 343 students in 13 regular science classrooms), the authors investigated differences between technology-based science classrooms and regular science classrooms in terms of students' attitudes and classroom environment perceptions using MANOVA and effect sizes. For the seven attitude and learning environment scales for which differences between technology-based and regular science classes were statistically significant (Attitudes to Computers, Self-regulation, Investigation, Task Orientation, Collaboration, Computer Usage and Formative Assessment), the effect sizes were 0.37, 0.31, 0.36, 0.40, 0.22, 1.09 and 0.27 standard deviations, respectively. For all of these scales, scores were higher in technology-based science classrooms, thus supporting the efficacy of technology-based science instruction among gifted female students.

Chapter 3 - More than 50 years ago, Margaret Mead and Rhoda Metráux surveyed 35,000 students to explore their views of science and scientists. Their study revealed that students held very different *personal* to *public* views, and that despite acknowledging the importance of science, attitudes towards personal engagement in science or with scientists, was generally negative. Later work by researchers such as Chambers (1983), Finson, Beaver and Cramond (1995), and Finson (2002) confirmed this to be an enduring issue, as revealed through studies using instruments such as the *Draw a Scientist Test (DAST)* and the *Draw a Scientist Test Checklist (DAST-C)*. However, some researchers concerned with this issue point to the possible value of scientists working with teachers in school-scientist partnerships (SSPs) as means of addressing some of these negative views. This chapter reports methods and outcomes from a study that explored the impact of a six-month SSP involving a New Zealand science research institute and a group of 164, 9-10 year olds. It used the DAST-C, a short response questionnaire and semi-structured interviews, to investigate the influence of the partnership on students' views of science and scientists. Results suggest the partnership had some positive impact on students' existing stereotypical views that could be attributed to specific design features, but that other aspects of the partnership, such as how it was executed in the classroom, actually appeared to *reinforce* negative perceptions. Recommendations are made that it is hoped will provide guidance for designing and implementing similar initiatives.

Chapter 4 - Learning through discovery is seen as an effective tool to enable higher level learning by enabling students to move away from being audience and act more independently and actively within the classroom. The aim this study was to investigate the effects of learning boxes on the 5th grade students' academic achievement and retention in the science classes. In order to realize this aim, a quantitative research method including an experimental design was used. Students in the experimental group were taught through learning boxes during "let's solve our body puzzle" unit of the 5th grade science classes, while students in the control group were taught the same unit through the teaching activities framed in the national curriculum. The participants involved 48 (Experiment: 24, Control: 24) students attending a state secondary school in Diyarbakır-Çınar district during the fall semester of 2016-2017 academic year. The study revealed that students taught through discovery learning supported with learning boxes scored significantly higher in academic achievement in comparison with the participants in the control group after the 10 weeks of the experimental learning process. The post-test results showed a statistically significant difference between the male and the female participant students in experimental group. Developing tools used in science teaching in the form of learning boxes and integrating them into constructivist approaches is among suggestions of the research.

Chapter 5 - The aims of this research are, (i) to consider Kuhn's concept of how scientific revolution takes place based on individual elements or tenets of Nature of Science (NOS), and (ii) to explore the inter-relationships within the individual elements or tenets of nature of science (NOS), based on the dimensions of scientific knowledge in science learning, this study suggests that instruction according to the authors' Explicit Integrated NOS Map should include the tenets of NOS. The aspects of NOS that have been emphasized in recent science education reform documents disagree with the received views of common science. Additionally, it is valuable to introduce students at the primary level to some of the ideas developed by Kuhn. Key aspects of NOS are, in fact, good applications to the history of science through Kuhn's philosophy. Therefore, an Explicit Integrated NOS Flow Map could be a promising means of understanding the NOS tenets and an explicit and reflective tool for science teachers to enhance scientific teaching and learning.

In: Science Teaching and Learning
Editor: Paul J. Hendricks

ISBN: 978-1-53617-406-9
© 2020 Nova Science Publishers, Inc.

Chapter 1

STEM INTEGRATION: EVIDENCES OF STUDENTS' LEARNING

Mónica Baptista[*], Iva Martins and Teresa Conceição
Instituto de Educação da Universidade de Lisboa, Lisboa, Portugal

ABSTRACT

This chapter aims to analyse the students' learning, during the development of STEM activities, in the following categories: real-world problem solving, knowledge about the topic under discussion and design. This study is part of a larger project that comprised five school clusters, involving students from several grades. In this chapter, we have chosen to focus in one of the school clusters and in two STEM activities (color of our houses and dye wool). These activities were performed by 119 students belonging to 3rd and 4th grade. Both activities were designed considering the five dimensions described by Thibaut et al. (2018) and were planned in alignment with the national curriculum for the elementary school. Results show that students indeed understood scientific concepts (i.e., knowledge about the topic under discussion), as well as developed scientific competences through solving problems related with their local context by inquiry-based learning. The results also showed that the activities allowed students to apply scientific knowledge

---

[*] Corresponding Author's Email: mbaptista@ie.ulisboa.pt.

in building house replicas and manufacturing wool accessories (i.e., design). Additionally, in order to well-succeed on these actions, students had to work with others, communicating and negotiating meanings and positions, and confronting in a respectful manner others' ideas and positions. These are all important competencies that are commonly agreed that citizens should have.

Keywords: STEM integration, learning science, science education

INTRODUCTION

The existence of global problems and the complexity of the world in which we live, require citizens to develop various skills and abilities. International results, as OECD (2019), show that the development of citizens' global skills and, in particular, their scientific literacy, is crucial. However, international documents underlined that students tend to avoid science and technology-related areas of study (OECD 2016). Two of the main reasons are that the students perceived the science curriculum as being difficult and their interest and self-efficacy in these areas are low (Osborne, Simon, and Collins 2003; Sjøberg and Schreiner 2010). In answer to that, several studies suggest introducing students to STEM (Science, Technology, Engineering and Mathematics) curriculum integration. In fact, according to literature, STEM integration enables the promotion of students' curiosity about natural phenomena (Crippen and Antonenko 2018; Moore et al. 2015), the motivation for STEM areas and students' engagement in STEM disciplines, and the development of several competencies, namely problem solving, critical thinking and creativity (Guthrie, Wigfield and VonSecker 2000; Hurley 2001). Additionally, in their recent work, Stehle and Peters-Burton (2019) show that STEM provides environments that encourage the development of 21st Century Skills (Partnership for 21st Century Learning 2016), namely: knowledge construction, real-world problem solving, skilled communication, collaboration, use of information and communication technology for learning, and self-regulation.

STEM Integration: Evidences of Students' Learning 3

Besides the above-mentioned benefits, additional earnings concerning STEM integration are described. For instance, in a study performed by Lamb et al. (2012), with 254 students (ages from 5 to 12 years old), it was possible to confirm that a STEM curriculum had positive effects in students' self-efficacy and in their interest in STEM areas. In another study with 96 students belonging to 4th grade classes, Toma and Greca (2018) verified that an inquiry-based STEM education approach about simple machines, led to significantly more favorable attitudes about science. Similarly, Christensen and Knezek (2017) describe that more than 800 middle school students (aged from 10 to 14 years old) showed a positive interest in STEM areas after participating in a curricular STEM hands-on project. Furthermore, the authors concluded that there was an increase in students' intention to pursue a STEM career.

In informal contexts, it was revealed by Chittum et al. (2017) that a STEM program had a positive impact on middle school students in terms of their motivations and interest by STEM areas. Similarly, and also in an informal context, this same correlation was observed in a research performed by Shahali et al. (2017) with 242 high school students that participated in a STEM program. More recently, a research, conducted by Kitchen, Sonnert and Sadler (2018), showed that 845 high school students that participated in a summer program with a STEM approach, increased their intention to proceed a STEM career.

These results, although promising, must be cautiously interpreted. In fact, some studies revealed ambiguous findings in what concerns the learning of scientific concepts and students outcomes (Means et al. 2016; Saw 2018). Our study aims to fulfil some of the literature gaps, by analysing the students' learning, during the development of STEM activities, in the following categories: (1) real-world problem solving, (2) knowledge about the topic under discussion, and (3) design.

THEORETICAL FRAMEWORK

STEM education has been presented as an integral component of the 21st century curricula (National Research Council 2014), since it meets the skills that societies need. Actually, according to National Science and Technology Council (2013), the occupations of the future are STEM. So, it is important to attract students to pursue STEM-related careers (Christensen and Knezek 2017). Moreover, it has been recognized that even in non-related STEM careers, also require STEM knowledge and competencies (Bøe et al. 2011).

In the light of these circumstances, STEM literacy became an educational priority, to give an answer to the needs of societies (National Research Council 2014). According to the literature, STEM literacy is defined as the knowledge of the nature of STEM disciplines and the fluency in some of their central concepts, i.e., the understanding and application of conceptual, procedural and attitudinal content from the four STEM disciplines to solve real problems (Bybee 2010; National Research Council 2014; Zollman 2012).

STEM education has been subject to several considerations about what it means and how it can be integrated, since it cannot be perceived as a set of disconnected and independent contents from the four STEM areas. Johnson (2013, 367) defines STEM education as "an instructional approach, which integrates the teaching of science and mathematics disciplines through the infusion of the practices of scientific inquiry, technological and engineering design, mathematical analysis, and 21st century interdisciplinary themes and skills". In what concerns integrated STEM education, Nadelson and Seifert (2017, 221) define it as a fusion of concepts from the STEM disciplines with the integration occurring "in ways such that knowledge and process of specific STEM disciplines are considered simultaneously without regard to the discipline, but rather in the context of a problem, project or task". In a recent review, Martín-Páez et al. (2019) describes that the concept of "integrative STEM education" was created to define STEM education that integrates the four disciplines in an interdisciplinary manner. However, as described by the same authors, in their literature review about STEM education, besides this interdisciplinary concept, other conceptions of STEM education are found, which reveals the lack of consensus about what STEM education means and how the four STEM disciplines can be integrated.

According to Vasquez (2014, 12), "defining STEM is the easy part, implementing STEM education on a large scale is more challenging" and, hence, this author presents a comprehensive perspective about different levels of STEM integration, in a form of an inclined plane, from disciplinary to transdisciplinary, passing through multidisciplinary and interdisciplinary. At the bottom level of integration sits the disciplinary teaching, where students learn concepts and skills separately in each discipline. Along the illustrative inclined plane, the lines between STEM disciplines become more blurred, until it reaches a transdisciplinary integration, where the interconnection and interdependence among the disciplines is greater, and students apply knowledge and skills from two or more disciplines to real-world problems and projects.

In a similar perspective, Nadelson and Seifert (2017) describe the STEM spectrum raging from a segregated approach to an integrated STEM approach. The integrated STEM approach implies the application of knowledge and practices from the STEM disciplines, which allows students to develop a deeper understanding of STEM concepts and their interrelation. Moreover, these authors find context as being crucial for a successful integrated STEM approach, in the sense that enhances the meaningfulness and relevancy of the learning experience, increasing students' motivation and engagement. Furthermore, optimal STEM learning entails an alignment between the context and students' knowledge and learning ability. Likewise, as stated by Pilot and Bulte (2006), it is essential that the context of the real-world problems presented is relevant to the students and that a context-based approach "brings the learning of science closer to the life and interests of students" (Pilot and Bulte 2006, 953). In fact, it is important that a selected context allows students to realize "Why am I learning this?" (Roberts 1982, 245) and, according to Bennett, Lubben and Hogarth (2007), this improves students' attitudes, motivation and interest towards STEM disciplines.

Even with some insights of what is an integrated STEM approach, the question that remains unclear concerns the instructional principles that guide the implementation of an integrated STEM education. For instance, some authors reduce it to project-based learning, inquiry-based learning or design-based learning as appropriate STEM teaching methodologies (e.g., Lamb, Akmal, and Petrie 2015; Lou et al. 2017; Mustafa et al. 2016; Sanders 2009; Toma and Greca 2018), while others do not even make it explicit (Barret and Hegarty 2016; Gentile et al. 2012). For that reason, in a recent work, Thibaut et al. (2018) present a systematic review of literature concerning integrated STEM education and propose a well-defined framework for instructional practices. The proposed framework is supported in the social constructivist learning theory, that states that knowledge is actively constructed by students, based on their previous experiences and ideas, and that is a shared, rather than an individual experience. This theoretical framework comprises five key principles: (1) integration of STEM content, which must be explicit in order to help students to develop their knowledge and skills across the different STEM disciplines; (2) problem-centered learning, that is essential to involve students in meaningfulness authentic real-world problems; (3) inquiry-based learning, that allows students to be engaged in the different practices that enable them to solve the initial problem, to learn new concepts and to develop new skills through questioning, experimental learning and hands-on activities; (4) design-based learning, that implies engineering design challenges in order to deepen students' knowledge about disciplinary central ideas; and (5) cooperative learning that, through teamwork, collaboration and communication, promotes the strength of students' knowledge. As stated by the authors, the definition of these five complementary key principles ensures a specific and detailed description of instructional practices concerning an integrated STEM education (Thibaut et al. 2018).

METHODS

Context and Participants

This study is part of a larger project that comprised five school clusters, involving around 1000 students from several grades, ranging from elementary school to high school. In this chapter, we have chosen to focus in only one of the school clusters and in two STEM activities. These activities were performed by 119 students belonging to 3rd and 4th grade classrooms (54% girls, 46% boys, 8 to 10 years old). The students belong to the middle class and the school cluster is located about 200 km from Lisbon.

STEM Activities

STEM activities were planned in alignment with the national curriculum for the elementary school (ME 2004). In Portugal, science curriculum starts at the 1st grade and through the elementary school, i.e., until the 4th grade, students learn concepts and procedures from several subjects (History, Geography, Biology, Natural Sciences, etc.), which aims to contribute to a progressive comprehension of the inter-relations among Nature and Society. In particular, the activities described in this work, were implemented in the 3rd and 4th grades and focused on the light, namely the reflection and absorption of electromagnetic radiation ("The color of our houses") and types of materials ("How to dye wool?"). The activities lasted two classes of two hours each and involved group work inside and outside the school.

Both activities were designed taking in account the five dimensions described by Thibaut et al. (2018): integration of STEM content; problem-centered learning, inquiry-based learning, design-based learning; and cooperative learning.

The activity "The color of our houses" was proposed to the students because the region of Portugal where they live is known by the white house facades. In this sense, the activity was guided by an initial problem: "Why are the houses in our region white?" (problem-centered learning). In order to give an answer to this question, students explored the problem, formulated hypotheses, planned and performed experiences, registered their observations and drew conclusions (inquiry-based learning). At the end of the activity, the students mobilized the knowledge they developed during the activity to build a model of the houses of that region (design-based learning).

Besides the distinctive white houses, the region of Portugal where the school cluster is located has a tradition in the manufacturing of typical wool blankets. Thus, in the second activity the students had to answer the problem: "How to dye wool?" (problem-centered learning). To do that, the students formulated hypotheses, planned and performed experiences, registered observations and drew conclusions (inquiry-based learning). As a way of applying their knowledge, students built looms and made woolen items (design-based learning).

As it can be perceived, the proposed activities were designed taking into account the students' local context, to foster the students' situational interest by STEM and problem solving, as well as stimulate the relevance of the topic (i.e., the notion from students' perspective that scientific knowledge is useful to explain certain phenomena). Also, and as stated before, both activities were implemented in order to promote cooperative learning, i.e., during the activities students communicated and collaborated with each other, as a way to strengthen their knowledge.

Data Collection and Analysis

Students' written productions were collected. These documents were analysed, according to previous defined categories: (1) knowledge about the topic under discussion, (2) real-world problem solving, (3) design. Each one of the categories is described in Table 1.

Table 1. Data analysis categories

Category	Description
Knowledge about the topic under discussion	Students mobilize scientific knowledge for making sense of problems related with their daily life.
Real-world problem solving	Students solve problems related with their local context by inquiry-based learning (plan experiences, perform experiences, make observations, draw conclusions, etc.)
Design	Students are engaged in engineering design processes, applying and developing their knowledge about science, technology and mathematics

RESULTS

Activity "The Color of Our Houses"

Real-World Problem Solving

The activity "The color of our houses" aimed to led students to perform experiences about the light and to give them the opportunity to understand optical phenomena, like the reflection and absorption of the electromagnetic radiation. Thus, considering the problem under investigation "Why are the houses in our region white?", students were firstly asked to formulate hypotheses that could give an answer to the initial question. In this sense, one of the groups formulated the following hypothesis to be tested (Figure 1).

Despite the incorrect use of scientific terminology (i.e., misunderstanding between heat and temperature), the explanatory hypothesis formulated by the students is scientific exploitable. Considering their hypothesis, students performed a teacher-oriented internet search to collect information about experimental procedures that could be used to explore the formulated hypothesis. An example of planning is shown in Figure 2.

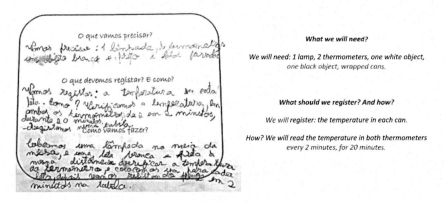

Figure 1. Example of a testable hypothesis formulated by a group of students.

Most of the houses are painted white because in this region, when it's hot, the white color makes the house fresh.

What we will need?

We will need: 1 lamp, 2 thermometers, one white object, one black object, wrapped cans.

What should we register? And how?

We will register: the temperature in each can.

How? We will read the temperature in both thermometers every 2 minutes, for 20 minutes.

Figure 2. Students' written document about planning an experience.

From this excerpt, it is possible to observe that students were able to plan an experiment, including the control of variables like the distance at which the cans are placed in relation to the lamp, the measurement of the initial temperature of each can, as well as the temperature control at defined times, in order to be able to compare the results.

Based on their planning, the students performed the activity (Figure 3) and collected the data (Figure 4).

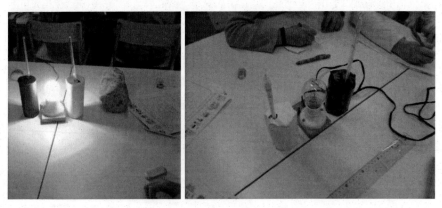

Figure 3. Apparatus of the performed experiment.

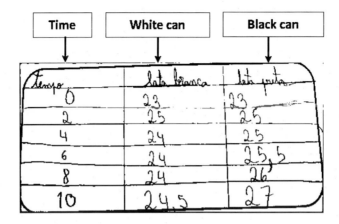

Figure 4. Students' written document about data registration.

Students registered the collected data in the form of a table, which allowed them to organize their observations and measurements and to use them to substantiate their positions, explanations and argumentation. However, some features of the table needed improvement, namely the indication of the measured variable (temperature), as well as its units (°C). Nevertheless, this registration allowed students to reach to a conclusion, as shown in Figure 5.

Based on the conclusion elaborated by the students, it can be seen that they were able to recognize a correlation between temperature variation and the color of the can: they found that the temperature does not change a lot when the can is white. They also related the higher temperature in the black can with the absorption of the radiation.

The temperature increased in both cans but more slowly in the white can. The temperature increase in the black can was higher. The black color absorbs more radiation, and that is why the temperature

Figure 5. Students' written document about the formulation of conclusions.

Knowledge about the Topic under Discussion

As described, this activity raised a question that led students to wonder why the houses in their region are predominantly white. Along the activity, students planned and executed an experiment in order to answer the question. Some of the conclusions written by the students are presented in Figure 6 and Figure 7.

The conclusion represents a fundamental stage in the accomplishment of any activity since it requires the mobilization of knowledge and, very often, the extrapolation of information. In fact, in these excerpts students reflected about their learning and it is evident that they understood that the temperature change is lower in the white can. Additionally, they were able to use scientific terms like "reflection" and "absorption" of light to justify their conclusions and, in one of the excerpts (Figure 7), students emphasize the need to control variables, namely the distance to the source of radiation. Finally, by extrapolation, they were able to conclude that the houses are white because there is a need to reflect part of the solar radiation, to keep them cooler.

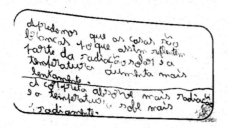

We learned that the houses are white because, in that way, they reflect the solar radiation and the temperature *raises more slowly*.

The black color absorbs more radiation and the temperature increases more radically.

Figure 6. Students' written document about the formulation of conclusions.

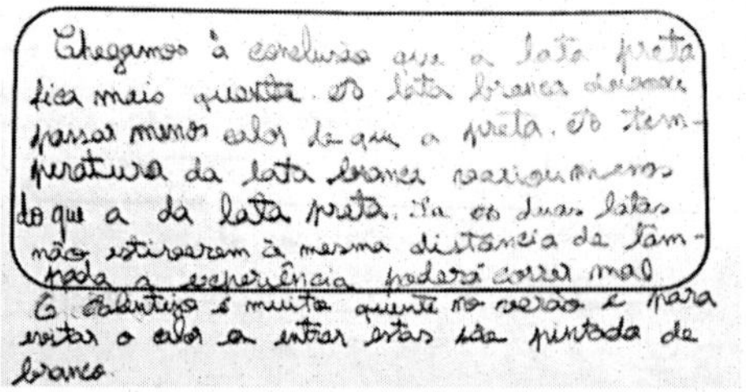

We concluded that the black can becomes hotter. The white let it pass less heat than the black can. The temperature of the white can vary less than the temperature of the black can. If the cans were not at the same distance from the lamp, the experience could go wrong.

This region is very hot in the Summer and to avoid the heat the houses are white painted.

Figure 7. Students' written document about the formulation of conclusions.

Design

In last part of the activity, students were asked to build models of the houses. To perform this task, students went on field trip (Figure 8) to see the typical local white houses *in loco* and to sense the differences in temperature, according to the color they were painted with.

Figure 8. Students in the field trip, sensing the difference in the temperatures of the houses.

Figure 9. An engineer helping students to design their models of the houses.

Following this task, a local engineer helped the students to design their replicas (Figure 9). The students were asked to apply their mathematic knowledge to understand the proportions of the houses, the areas, etc.

Finally, the students built their house models (Figure 10), applying the knowledge they developed along the activity.

Activity "How to Dye Wool"

Real-World Problem Solving

The second activity, "How to dye wool?", was related to the sheep wool which has a great tradition in that region of Portugal, namely in the manufacturing of colorful wool blankets. In what concerns the science curriculum, this activity allowed students to learn about natural and synthetic materials, like natural dyes (onion peel, sugar-beet and spinach) and commercial food coloring. Based on this context, the students were confronted with the initial problem "How to dye wool?" and an example of a testable hypothesis formulated by the students is presented in Figure 11.

Figure 10. The process of house models construction.

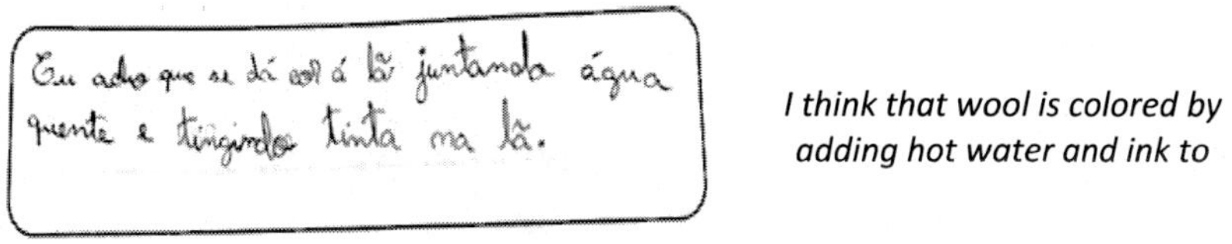

STEM Integration: Evidences of Students' Learning 15

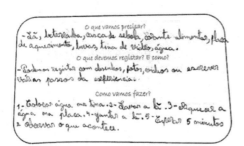

I think that wool is colored by adding hot water and ink to

Figure 11. Example of a hypothesis formulated by a student.

After formulating the hypotheses, the students made an oriented search on the internet about textile dyeing. Based on the collected information, students were able to plan an experiment (Figure 12), in order to dye the sheep wool provided by a local shepherd.

What we will need?

Wool, sugar-beet, onion peel, food coloring, heating plate, gloves, glass container, water.

What should we register? And how?

We can register with drawings, photos, videos or write down the several steps of the experience.

Figure 12. Students' written document about planning an experience.

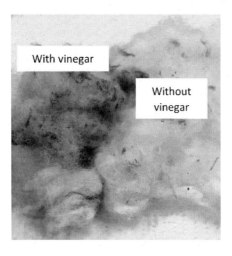

Figure 13. Effect of vinegar addition in color fixation.

In this planning, it is evident that students have learned how to plan an experimental activity and explain, step by step, the procedure. In the presented example, students choose to use two natural dyes (sugar-beet and onion peel) and artificial dyes, performed the experience according to their plan and realized that there was no color fixation to the wool, unless they used vinegar (Figure 13).

After reformulating the experimental procedure, students were able to dye the wool, using both natural and synthetic dyes. Some of the experiment steps are illustrated in Figure 14.

Figure 14. Wool dyeing with natural and artificial dyes.

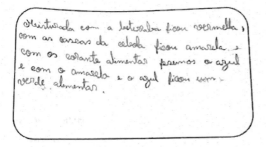

Mixing with the sugar-beet (the wool) became red, with the onion peels became yellow and with the blue food coloring became blue and with the yellow and blue became green.

Figure 15. Students' written document about their observations.

STEM Integration: Evidences of Students' Learning   17

-The yellow wool was made with onion.

-The green wool was made with detergent.

- The red wool was made with sugar-beet.

Figure 16. Students' written document about their observations.

Along the experience, students registered their observations, either by writing down their annotations (Figure 15) or drawing what they observed (Figure 16).

Knowledge about the Topic under Discussion

In this experimental activity students were able to plan and perform wool coloring, using different dyes. This allowed students to conclude that the materials could be classified as natural and synthetic and that, in the presented context, both natural and synthetic dyes could be used to dye the wool, as stated in the following conclusion (Figure 17).

Design

In order to complete the activity, students were asked to manufacture some wool accessories. To achieve this goal, students had to build small looms (Figure 18) to weave the wool.

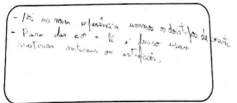

-In the experiment we used two kinds of dyes.

-To dye the wool, we needed natural or artificial materials.

Figure 17. Students' written document about the formulation of conclusions.

This part of the activity was also used to explore mathematic patterns, which are essential for students to develop their ability to classify and organize information. Thus, while weaving, students defined repeated sequences that were the base for their final products and, in this manner, they were able to understand the connection between mathematics and the real world (Figure 19).

Figure 18. Students weaving the wool.

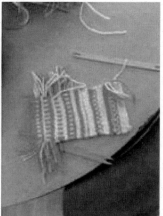

Figure 19. Wool patterns made by the students.

CONCLUSION

We live in a highly complex, changeable, and knowledge-based society. Actually, it is a society immersed in knowledge, because knowledge is the raw material on which we operate (i.e., which we transform) and it is simultaneously the means used for operating on that very raw material. This requires from citizens constant learning, i.e., new knowledge production, while using it to make sense of new situations and to solve problems.

In this society the importance of developing competent citizens is gained strength, i.e., citizens that are able to be creatives, to use critical thinking, to solve problems, to collaborate with others, to use technology, to become workers who can for example create new products, manage projects, lead others and produce results, to analyse, synthesize and share information from multiple sources, to communicate in a wide variety of forms and contexts (Beers 2011). Moreover, answer to the demands of this society require that citizens demonstrate their knowledge of science, technology, mathematics and engineering in a variety of ways (Ejiwale 2012). So, it is crucial that students in the school have to face learning situations that facilitate the STEM integration. And in fact, this study reveals that the two STEM activities, related to the local context of the students- "The color of our houses" and "How to dye wool" - and constructed according the model of STEM integration of the Thibaut et al. (2018), were important means for students, from 3rd and 4th grade, develop their learning. In fact, results showed that students indeed understood scientific concepts (i.e., knowledge about the topic under discussion), as well as developed scientific competences through solving problems related with their local context by inquiry-based learning. The results also showed that the design allowed students to fill the gap between scientific knowledge, abstract knowledge and application (Thibaut et al. 2018) because they had opportunity to apply the scientific concepts that they have learned in the building of house replicas and manufacturing some wool accessories (Ting 2016). In fact, both activities involved the analysis of problematic situations, related with color of our houses and the dye wool, which required from the students a number of diversified actions, such as: to formulate hypotheses; to search important information and to select the main relevant ideas for answering initial triggering situations; to plan and perform experiences; to make conclusions based on knowledge; to apply that information and scientific knowledge in order to build houses and manufacture wool accessories.

Additionally, in order to well-succeed on these actions, students had to work with others, communicating and negotiating meanings and positions, and confronting in a respectful manner others' ideas and positions. These are all important competencies that are commonly agreed that citizens should have (Bybee 2010). It is also possible to conclude that the two activities, given their characteristics (as referred the activities were constructed using the framework of Thibaut et al. 2018), were crucial to for motivation students to learn about the topics reflection and absorption of electromagnetic radiation and types of materials.

REFERENCES

Barrett, Trevor J. & Mary, Hegarty. (2016). "Effects of Interface and Spatial Ability on Manipulation of Virtual Models in a STEM Domain." *Computers in Human Behavior*, *65*, 220–31. https://doi.org/10.1016/j.chb.2016.06.026.

Beers, Sue Z. (2011). "What Are the Skills Students Will Need in the 21 St Century?". https://cosee.umaine.edu/files/coseeos/21st_century_skills.pdf.

Bennett, Judith., Fred, Lubben. & Sylvia, Hogarth. (2007). "Becoming a Scientist: The Role of Undergraduate Research in Students' Cognitive, Personal, and Professional Development." *Science Education*, *91* (1), 36–74. https://doi.org/10.1002/sce.

Bøe, Maria Vetleseter., Ellen, Karoline Henriksen., Terry, Lyons. & Camilla, Schreiner. (2011). "Participation in Science and Technology: Young People's Achievement-Related Choices in Late-Modern

Societies." *Studies in Science Education, 47* (1), 37–72. https://doi.org/10.1080/03057267.2011.549621.

Bybee, Rodger W. (2010). "Advancing STEM Education. A 2020 Vision." *Technology and Engineering Teacher, 70* (1), 30–35.

Chittum, Jessica R., Brett, D. Jones., Sehmuz, Akalin. & Ásta, B. Schram. (2017). "The Effects of an Afterschool STEM Program on Students' Motivation and Engagement." *International Journal of STEM Education, 4* (1). https://doi.org/10.1186/s40594-017-0065-4.

Christensen, Rhonda. & Gerald, Knezek. (2016). "Relationship of Middle School Student STEM Interest to Career Intent." *Journal of Education in Science, Environment and Health, 3* (1), 1–1. https://doi.org/10.21891/jeseh.275649.

Crippen, Kent. & Pavlo, "Pasha" Antonenko. (2018). "Designing for Collaborative Problem Solving in STEM Cyberlearning." In *Cognition, Metacognition, and Culture in STEM Education, Innovation in Science Education and Technology*, edited by Yehudit Judy Dori, Zemira Mevarech, and Dale Baker, 89–116. Weston, MA: Springer International Publishing.

Ejiwale, James A. (2012). "Facilitating Teaching and Learning Across STEM Fields." *Journal of STEM Education: Innovations and Research, 13* (3), 87–94.

Gentile, Lisa., Lester, Caudill., Mirela, Fetea., April, Hill., Kathy, Hoke., Barry, Lawson., Ovidiu, Lipan., et al. (2012). "Challenging Disciplinary Boundaries in the First Year: Integrated Science Course for STEM Majors." *Journal of College Science Teaching, 41* (5), 44–50.

Guthrie, John T., Allan, Wigfield. & Clare, VonSecker. (2000). "Effects of Integrated Instruction on Motivation and Strategy Use in Reading." *Journal of Educational Psychology, 92* (2), 331–41. https://doi.org/10.1037/0022-0663.92.2.331.

Hurley, Marlene M. (2001). "Reviewing Integrated Science and Mathematics: The Search for Evidence and Definitions From New Perspectives." *School Science and Mathematics, 101* (5), 259–68. https://doi.org/10.1111/j.1949-8594.2001.tb18028.x.

Johnson, Carla C. (2013). "Conceptualizing Integrated STEM Education." *School Science and Mathematics*, *113* (8), 367–68.

Kitchen, Joseph A., Gerhard, Sonnert. & Philip, M. Sadler. (2018). "The Impact of College- and University-Run High School Summer Programs on Students' End of High School STEM Career Aspirations." *Science Education*, *102* (3), 529–47. https://doi.org/ 10.1002/sce.21332.

Lamb, Richard Lawrence., Leonard, Annetta., Jeannette, Meldrum. & David, Vallett. (2012). "Measuring Science Interest: Rasch Validation of the Science Interest Survey." *International Journal of Science and Mathematics Education*, *10*, 643–68.

Lamb, Richard., Tariq, Akmal. & Kaylan, Petrie. (2015). "Development of a Cognition-Priming Model Describing Learning in a STEM Classroom." *Journal of Research in Science Teaching*, *52* (3), 410–37. https://doi.org/10.1002/tea.21200.

Lou, Shi Jer., Yung, Chieh Chou., Ru, Chu Shih. & Chih, Chao Chung. (2017). "A Study of Creativity in CaC 2 Steamship-Derived STEM Project-Based Learning." *Eurasia Journal of Mathematics*, *Science and Technology Education*, *13* (6), 2387–2404. https://doi.org/ 10.12973/ EURASIA.2017.01231A.

Martín-Páez, Tobías., David, Aguilera., Francisco, Javier Perales-Palacios. & José, Miguel Vílchez-González. (2019). "What Are We Talking about When We Talk about STEM Education? A Review of Literature." *Science Education*, *103* (4), 799–822. https://doi.org/ 10.1002/sce.21522.

Means, Barbara., Haiwen, Wang., Viki, Young., Vanessa, L. Peters. & Sharon, J. Lynch. (2016). "STEM-Focused High Schools as a Strategy for Enhancing Readiness for Postsecondary STEM Programs." *Journal of Research in Science Teaching*, *53* (5), 709–36. https://doi.org/ 10.1002/tea.21313.

ME. (2004). *1º Ciclo Ensino Básico. Organização Curricular e Programas*. Lisboa: Ministério da Educação. [Ministry of Education. 2004. *1st Cycle Basic Learning. Curricular Organization and Programs*. Lisbon: Ministry of Education].

Moore, Tamara J., Kristina, M. Tank., Aran, W. Glancy. & Jennifer, A. Kersten. (2015). "NGSS and the Landscape of Engineering in K-12 State Science Standards." *Journal of Research in Science Teaching, 52* (3), 296–318. https://doi.org/10.1002/tea.21199.

Mustafa, Norazla., Zaleha, Ismail., Zaidatun, Tasir. & Mohd, Nihra Haruzuan Mohamad Said. (2016). "A Meta-Analysis on Effective Strategies for Integrated STEM Education." *Advanced Science Letters, 22* (12), 4225–88. https://doi.org/10.1166/asl.2016.8111.

Nadelson, Louis S. & Anne, L. Seifert. (2017). "Integrated STEM Defined: Contexts, Challenges, and the Future." *Journal of Educational Research, 110* (3), 221–23. https://doi.org/10.1080/00220671.2 017.1289775.

Nadelson, Louis S. & Anne, L. Seifert. (2017). "Integrated STEM Defined: Contexts, Challenges, and the Future." *Journal of Educational Research, 110* (3), 221–23. https://doi.org/10.1080/00220671.20 17.1289775.

National Research Council. (2014). *STEM Integration in K-12 Education: Status, Prospects, and an Agenda for Research. STEM Integration in K-12 Education: Status, Prospects, and an Agenda for Research.* Washington DC: The National Academies Press. https://doi.org/ 10.17226/18612.

National Science and Technology Council. (2013). "*Federal Science, Technology, Engineering, and Mathematics (STEM) Education. 5 Year Strategic Plan.A Report from the Committee on STEM Education.*" Washington DC.

OECD. (2016). *Education at a Glance 2016: OECD Indicators.* Paris: OECD Publishing. https://doi.org/https://doi.org/10.1787/eag-2016-en.

OECD. (2019). *Education at a Glance 2019: OECD Indicators.* Paris: OECD Publishing. https://doi.org/https://doi.org/10.1787/ea8ba064-en.

Osborne, Jonathan., Shirley, Simon. & Sue, Collins. (2003). "Attitudes towards Science: A Review of the Literature and Its Implications." *International Journal of Science Education, 25* (9), 1049–79. https:// doi.org/10.1080/0950069032000032199.

Partnership for 21st Century Learning. (2016). "*Framework for 21st Century Learning.*" 2016. www.p21.org/about-us/p21-framework.

Pilot, Albert. & Astrid, Bulte. (2006). "Why Do You 'Need to Know'? Context-Based Education." *International Journal of Science Education, 28* (9), 953–56. https://doi.org/10.1080/0950069060 0702462.

Roberts, Douglas A. (1982). "Developing the Concept of 'Curriculum Emphases' in Science Education." *Science Education, 66* (2), 243–60.

Sanders, M. (2009). "STEM, STEM Education, STEMmania." *The Technology Teacher, 68* (4), 20–27.

Saw, Guan. (2019). "The Impact of Inclusive STEM High Schools on Student Outcomes: A Statewide Longitudinal Evaluation of Texas STEM Academies." *International Journal of Science and Mathematics Education, 17* (8), 1445–57. https://doi.org/10.1007/s10763-018-09942-3.

Shahali, Edy Hafizan Mohd., Lilia, Halim., Mohamad, Sattar Rasul., Kamisah, Osman. & Mohd, Afendi Zulkifeli. (2017). "STEM Learning through Engineering Design: Impact on Middle Secondary Students' Interest towards STEM." *Eurasia Journal of Mathematics, Science and Technology Education, 13* (5), 1189–1211. https://doi.org/10.12973/eurasia.2017.00667a.

Sjøberg, Svein. & Camilla, Schreiner. (2010). *The ROSE Project. An Overview and Key Findings.* Oslo: Univeristy of Oslo.

Stehle, Stephanie M. & Erin, E. Peters-Burton. (2019). "Developing Student 21st Century Skills in Selected Exemplary Inclusive STEM High Schools." *International Journal of STEM Education, 6* (1), 39. https://doi.org/10.1186/s40594-019-0192-1.

Thibaut, Lieve., Stijn, Ceuppens., Haydée, De Loof., Jolien, De Meester., Leen, Goovaerts., Annemie, Struyf., Jelle, Boeve-de Pauw., et al. (2018). "Integrated STEM Education: A Systematic Review of Instructional Practices in Secondary Education." *European Journal of STEM Education, 3* (1), 1–12. https://doi.org/10.20897/ejsteme/85525.

Ting, Yu-Liang. (2016). "STEM from the Perspectives of Engineering Design and Suggested Tools and Learning Design." *Journal of Research in STEM Education*, 2 (1), 59–71.

Toma, Radu Bogdan. & Ileana, M. Greca. (2018). "The Effect of Integrative STEM Instruction on Elementary Students' Attitudes toward Science." *Eurasia Journal of Mathematics, Science and Technology Education*, *14* (4), 1383–95. https://doi.org/10.29333/ejmste/83676.

Vasquez, Jo Anne. (2014). "STEM- Beyond the Acronym." *Educational Leadership: Journal of the Department of Supervision and Curriculum Development, N.E.A*, *70* (4), 10–16.

Zollman, Alan. (2012). "Learning for STEM Literacy: STEM Literacy for Learning." *School Science and Mathematics*, *112* (1), 12–19. https://doi.org/10.1111/j.1949-8594.2012.00101.x.

In: Science Teaching and Learning
Editor: Paul J. Hendricks

ISBN: 978-1-53617-406-9
© 2020 Nova Science Publishers, Inc.

Chapter 2

TECHNOLOGY-BASED SCIENCE TEACHING AMONG GIFTED FEMALES IN SINGAPORE: ATTITUDES AND LEARNING ENVIRONMENT

G. Sundari Pramathevan and Barry J. Fraser
Curtin University, Perth, Australia

ABSTRACT

This science education study was the first in Singapore to focus on gifted female students in technology-based classrooms in a secondary-school setting. We developed, validated and used an attitude and learning environment questionnaire for gifted female students to evaluate technology-based science instruction by comparing regular and technology-based science classrooms. This questionnaire contains four attitude scales (Attitudes to Computers, Task Value, Self-efficacy and Self-regulation) and six learning environment scales (Investigation, Task Orientation, Collaboration, Differentiation, Computer Usage and Formative Assessment). For our sample of 722 students (379 students in 14 technology-based science classrooms and 343 students in 13 regular science classrooms), we investigated differences between technology-based science classrooms and regular science classrooms in terms of students' attitudes and classroom environment perceptions using MANOVA and effect sizes. For the seven attitude and learning environment scales for which differences between technology-based and regular science classes were statistically significant (Attitudes to Computers, Self-regulation, Investigation, Task Orientation, Collaboration, Computer Usage and Formative Assessment), the effect sizes were 0.37, 0.31, 0.36, 0.40, 0.22, 1.09 and 0.27 standard deviations, respectively. For all of these scales, scores were higher in technology-based science classrooms, thus supporting the efficacy of technology-based science instruction among gifted female students.

Keywords: attitudes, gifted education, girls in science, learning environment, science education, secondary education, Singapore, technology-based teaching

INTRODUCTION

Although there is plenty of research literature and biographical and anecdotal accounts about gifted learners, there have been few studies of the experiences of gifted female students in science learning environments and even fewer of the attitudes of gifted students in science classrooms. Therefore, we undertook the present study among gifted secondary science students in Singapore with the main aim of evaluating the effectiveness of a technology-based one-student one-laptop program in terms of students' attitudes and their perceptions of the classroom learning environment.

This chapter is divided into four main sections. First, a comprehensive literature review encompasses the history of gifted education and the approach to gifted education in Singapore. Second, the context of our study is clarified in terms of the current education system in Singapore and the science curriculum for gifted Singaporean students. The third section is devoted to our study's research methods and includes: a pilot study; the sample and instructional methods; the student attitude scales selected; and the learning environment scales used. Fourth results are reported for our comparative evaluation of the effectiveness of technology-based instruction for gifted students in terms of student attitudes and the classroom learning environment.

LITERATURE REVIEW ON GIFTED EDUCATION

Our main purpose was to assess the effectiveness of using technology among gifted girls in science classrooms by investigating differences between technology-based science classrooms and regular classrooms in terms of students' attitudes and perceptions of classroom learning environment. Therefore, this section provides a detailed review of literature on gifted education, including a historical perspective on giftedness and details of provisions for gifted education specifically in Singapore.

History of Giftedness and Gifted Education

Giftedness was recognised long before the nineteenth century in ancient civilisations such as those in China, Turkey, Rome and Greece, with the brightest people in these societies being identified and groomed for leadership positions (Silverman, 2013). During those early centuries, conceptions of giftedness were not confined to general academic abilities and talents in specific areas such as aesthetics, science and economics, but they also included physical ability as a desirable 'gift'. Because military skills were highly valued in ancient Sparta, all boys at the age of seven years were trained in combat and warfare. Greek boys of upper social class were favoured in Athens and sent to private schools to learn reading, writing, arithmetic, history, literature, the arts and physical fitness.

The first person to study giftedness scientifically was Englishman Francis Galton, whose book *Hereditary Genius* created controversy and a breakthrough that spurred more research in later years. Galton stated that intelligence was inherited through natural selection and his *Inquiries into Human Faculty* in 1883 explored the possibility of measuring intelligence. A year later, he created the first mental tests which were measures of sensory capacity (Boring, 1950). The psychology of individual differences and the quantitative analysis of human intelligence were two of the many legacies of Galton (Silverman, 2013).

Alfred Binet and Victor Henri published an original paper in 1896 entitled 'Individual Psychology' which concluded that differentiating normal individuals from gifted people using their sensory capacities was less reliable than using higher intellectual processes. Therefore, they proposed a series of simple tests to assess mental capacities such as memory, imagination, understanding and will power. Binet and Henri's work was the first step towards the creation of the first intelligence scale (Binet & Simon, 1905) for measuring intelligence as a single numerical outcome.

In 1908, Henry Herbert Goddard, who was greatly influenced by Francis Galton's seminal work on geniuses, traveled from America to Europe to study with Binet in France and learn about Binet-Simon measurement scales. He was the first to translate the test into English, use it with mentally-retarded children in schools, popularise it by distributing it to American educators and psychologists, and advocate its use in public schools throughout the United States (Zenderland, 1998).

Whilst Goddard is regarded as the 'father' of intelligence testing in the United States, Lewis Terman is known as the 'father' of the gifted education movement. Terman modified the original Binet-Simon intelligence test into the Stanford-Binet test in 1916, and subsequently revised it in 1937 and 1960 to suit the American population, thereby changing intelligence testing and the face of American education. Terman adopted from the German psychologist, William Stern, a definition of 'intelligence quotient' (also known as the 'IQ') as the ratio between mental and chronological age multiplied by 100 (Sattler, 1992).

In 1939, David Wechsler, another American psychologist, proposed a different form of measuring intelligence because he felt that the previous instruments placed too much emphasis on verbal capacity and ignored other vital attributes. His Wechsler-Bellevue test became popular, widely accepted and extensively used for assessing intelligence in the USA. He revised the test in 1942 and published the Wechsler Intelligence Scale for Children (Wechsler, 1949), which was updated in 1974.

In 1915, Terman's paper entitled 'The Mental Hygiene of Exceptional Children' proposed that, although giftedness is inherited, it requires nurturing to reach its potential and, for this, schools should cater for the development of children with exceptional intelligence (Bernreuter, Miles, Tinker, & Young, 1942). He is also well known for initiating the longitudinal study of children with high IQs called the 'Genetic Studies of Genius' in 1921. Terman tracked children with extremely high IQs in childhood throughout their lives to ascertain if they had successful adult lives. Any child with an IQ above 140, which was deemed to be the highest intellectual range, was identified as gifted (Colangelo & Davis, 2003). Terman claimed that unusually precocious children are more likely to be generally successful in their careers and that many receive awards in recognition of their achievement, thus dispelling the contrary opinion that gifted children are unwell and social misfits. Although many gifted children in Terman's study did exceptionally well in their adulthood, the fact that some did not was attributed by Terman to potential talent not being realised, lack of opportunity, personal obstacles and education (Terman, 1925).

Before Galton's *Hereditary Genius* was published in 1869, William Torrey Harris, superintendent of public schools for St. Louis, introduced education for the gifted and allowed rapid advancement through the curriculum every five weeks based on academic performance. Between the periods of 1901 to 1956, very few special schools and classes were started to support the education of gifted students, with most of these being spearheaded by Hollingworth, who also published the first textbook on gifted education entitled *Gifted Children: Their Nature and Nurture* (National Association for Gifted Children, 2008). Studies of giftedness in the nineteenth century by Galton and Binet and early twentieth century by pioneers such as Lewis Terman and Leta Hollingworth brought scientific credibility to the field of gifted education, together with the realisation that existing school systems were not adequately meeting the needs of all children.

Strong interest in gifted education was fueled again in the United States in 1957 by the launching of Russia's satellite, Sputnik, when large amounts of money were channeled into identifying the brightest and most-talented students for studying advanced mathematics, science and technology. This was short-lived because, in 1964, the Civil Rights Act placed emphasis on equal education for all. The next wave of interest in gifted education started in 1972 following the Marland Report, the first national report on gifted education by the USA Department of Education to the Congress of the United States, which claimed that gifted children are deprived and can suffer psychological damage and permanent impairment of their abilities. The report presented to the United States Congress urged schools to define giftedness broadly and provide adequate educational services to the gifted (Colangelo & Davis, 2003).

In 1974, the Office of the Gifted and Talented housed within the U.S. Office of Education was given official status. Interest in catering for the educational needs of gifted and talented children heightened in the mid-1970s when funds were set aside to identify gifted children and to design and formalise an enriched and accelerated curriculum. However, in 1975, the Education for All Handicapped Children Act established a federal mandate to serve children with special educational needs, but this did not include children with gifts and talents. Up until the early 1980s, the gifted movement took a step backwards because of the notion of equity, budget cuts and a lack of supportive teachers and administrators.

In 1983, the national report *A Nation at Risk* identified that America's brightest were not doing as well as their international contemporaries. This report suggested policies and practices in gifted education and advocated specially-tailored programs for the gifted.

Gifted education in Russia began in 1958 soon after the success of its space program. That year, the first physics and mathematics school was opened in Moscow (Yurkevich & Davidovich, 2009). Provision for the gifted in Israel began in 1973 when the Minister of Education recognised that each child had the right to develop his/her abilities and that it was the Ministry's responsibility to conceptualise the framework and content to cater for the development of these bright children (Burg, 1992). Although there were isolated attempts by different Australian states to provide special education for the academically gifted in the 1970s, it was not until the late 1990s that gifted education policies based on credible educational and psychological theories were established and when programs for the gifted and talented were carefully planned and implemented in schools (Gross, 1999). By 1990s, the U.S. government enacted legislation and allocated funds for initiating educational programs and services for gifted children and providing content standards, curriculum and assessment for challenging gifted children.

Gifted Education in Singapore

When Hollingworth (1940) extensively researched gifted children, she concluded that "the development of all the world's natural resources depends on human intelligence, courage, stamina and will. It depends primarily on *thinking*. Therefore, intellectually-gifted children are among the most valuable assets of a civilised nation" (p. 116). Because Singapore is a small nation with no physical natural resources, its economic and financial stability relies largely on its people. Therefore, since the country gained independence from Malaysia, its focus has been on educating its people. Although the education system in Singapore was first designed to provide children with a basic education so that they could contribute to the economy of the country, the New Education System was introduced in 1979 to provide opportunities to develop every child's potential to the limits of his or her abilities (National Library Board, 2016). Therefore, the Ministry designs and provides an education which is sound and relevant and which allows students to develop individually and reach their potential.

With the New Education System in place, there were concerns that the needs of intellectually-bright pupils were not being met and that their potential was not being realised within the existing curriculum framework. In 1981, when a group of educators led by the then Minister of Education visited Russia, Israel and West Germany to study their gifted programs, they found that the Israeli model of having special classes within regular schools was the best fit for Singapore. A program was proposed for the intellectually gifted for developing higher-level thinking skills, self-directed learning, social responsibility and civic awareness (National Library Board, 2015).

In 1984, the highly-selective Gifted Education Program (GEP) began in Singapore schools to identify the 0.5% of students who were the most outstanding from each academic year level. In Singapore, students are identified for the GEP based on their performance in selection tests, which are conducted at the end of grade 3. Students first take a screening test comprising English Language and Mathematics. About 4000 pupils are shortlisted for the GEP Selection Test comprising English Language, Mathematics and General Ability. Around 500 students are admitted into the GEP which is introduced in grade 4. These students have high intellectual ability and potential and so the curriculum is enriched and differentiated to cater for their development. This advanced curriculum is built on the regular curriculum, with the main advantage of the GEP being that it offers individualised enrichment and attention to gifted students. In grade 6, GEP students take the same Primary School Leaving Examination (PSLE) as mainstream students and are allocated to secondary schools based on their scores. Most students gain admission into the best secondary schools.

Besides developing "intellectual rigour, humane values and creativity in gifted youths" (Ministry of Education, 2016b, para. 6), one of the main reasons for implementing the GEP in Singapore is socio-political. It is considered advantageous for gifted children to be nurtured for "responsible leadership and service to country and society" (Ministry of Education, 2016b, para. 6). In Singapore, the goals of the GEP are: intellectual depth and higher-level thinking; productive creativity; attitudes for self-directed lifelong learning; aspirations for individual excellence and fulfilment; a strong social conscience and commitment to serve society and nation; and moral values and qualities for responsible leadership (Ministry of Education, 2016b, para. 6). Overall, the goal of the GEP is to equip pupils with the intellectual tools and attitudes to cope with the challenges of a fast-changing society in which they are likely to assume leadership roles, as well as to develop their values and abilities so that they can be at the forefront for the betterment of society (Quek, 1997).

SINGAPORE CONTEXT

To contextualise our study for readers, this section reviews literature concerning Singapore's education system and the science curriculum for gifted Singaporean students.

Current Education System in Singapore

Singapore has a strong education system that aims to help its "students to discover their own talents, to make the best of these talents and realise their full potential, and to develop a passion for learning that lasts through life" (Ministry of Education, 2016a, para. 1). It is hoped that a person who has been part of the Singapore education system will be confident, a self-directed learner, an active contributor and a concerned citizen, and to have a good sense of self-awareness, a sound moral compass, and the skills and knowledge required to take on the challenges of the future. Therefore, instead of focusing only on developing the academic potential of students, education also emphasises developing the skills, character and values that enable students to take the country forward in the future.

In recent years, changes have been made to the Singaporean education system to make it more flexible and diverse, to meet students' different interest and styles of learning, and to promote a diversity of talents. Students now have a wider choice of what and how they want to learn. A broad-based education system is also provided to ensure holistic development of the person to deal with ambiguities in the future (Ministry of Education, 2016a).

It is compulsory for Singaporean children to attend primary school. Although the pre-school years are not compulsory, many parents enrol their children in pre-schools to ensure that they are ready for primary education. Therefore, pre-school and primary education for a typical child in Singapore consists of: pre-school for children between the ages of 3 to 5 years; kindergarten for children between the ages 5 to 6 years; lower primary 1 to 3 (grade 1 to 3) for children between the ages 7 to 9 years;

and upper primary 4 to 6 (grade 4 to 6) for children between the ages 10 to 12 years.

At the secondary-school level, three courses are offered. Based on the child's Primary School Leaving Examination (PSLE) performance in Primary 6 (Grade 6), he/she is placed in the Express Course (including an Integrated Program in selected schools), the Normal (Academic) Course or Normal (Technical) Course. Although children might start with a particular secondary course based on their current abilities, learning pace and learning styles, there are opportunities for lateral transfer mid-stream to a more-suitable course that brings out their potential.

From 2004 onwards, the Integrated Program (IP) was introduced in a few high-ranking public and independent secondary schools. This six-year program provides secondary students who are academically bright with a seamless education for advancing into pre-university institutions without taking the 'O' level examination. These students have more time and flexibility for engaging in broader learning experiences during their secondary and pre-university years. At the end of the sixth year, students take the 'A' level examination or the International Baccalaureate.

The secondary school involved in our study is a specialised independent school and one of the highest-ranking girls' schools identified by the Ministry of Education in 2004 for offering its own IP. The aim is to use the time saved, which would have been otherwise used in preparing for the 'O' levels, to stretch its pupils and provide a more holistic curriculum in both academic and non-academic areas. The school conducts its own school-based assessments to monitor its pupils' progress. Students are admitted to this school based on their high scores in the Primary School Leaving Examinations and a direct-admission exercise conducted by the school. These students are among the top 1% to 3% of their cohort in terms of their performance. Thirty percent of the students admitted are also from the Gifted Education Program in their primary schools and, because students are high-ability learners, the school adopts the Integrated Curriculum Model for the gifted (Van Tassel-Baska, 1986).

Science Curriculum for Gifted Students in Singapore

Although most educational institutions focus on developing intellectually-gifted students, Van Tassel-Baska (2003) highlighted that the overriding trait of intellectually-gifted people is that they are developmentally advanced in language and thought. Consequently, she describes precocity, intensity and complexity as three characteristics relevant to curriculum planning for the gifted and talented. Essentially, the definition of giftedness adopted by an educational institution largely determines the procedures used in identification of the gifted, the curriculum and programming, teacher training and administrative support.

Science is a discipline that naturally promotes the curiosity and intellectual spirit of gifted students since their early years. However, this early interest in science is rarely matched with an appropriate curriculum within the school context (Van Tassel-Baska & Stambaugh, 2006). The National Commission on Excellence in Education (1983) reported that, during the previous 15 years, students had not been achieving well in science, with problems including poor take-up rates of advanced courses which are frequently not being offered in many secondary schools (Bybee, 1994; National Science Board Commission on Precollege Education in Mathematics, 1983) and girls and minority student dropping out of the science track as early as possible (Hilton, Hsia, Solorzano, & Benton, 1989). Also science was taught through the use of texts that emphasised reading and guided experiments rather than active learning (Lockwood, 1992a, 1992b). To improve the quality of teaching and learning of science, the American Association for the Advancement of Science's Project 2061 published benchmarks of science literacy goals and the National Research Council published a set of national education science standards since 1990s (Van Tassel-Baska & Stambaugh, 2006).

The Ministry of Education of Singapore designs the science syllabus which extends from the primary to the pre-university levels, with the syllabus at the lower levels providing a bridge and foundation for the pursuit of scientific studies at upper levels. This syllabus is based on a Science Curriculum Framework that provides a balance between the acquisition of science knowledge, skills and attitudes, as well as technological applications, social implications and the value aspects of science (Ministry of Education, 2016c). The science syllabus for gifted students is made more advanced to match their intellectual abilities. Although the same topics are taught, they are differentiated to include more depth and breadth in content. As a result, assessments for the gifted include more higher-order thinking than for mainstream students.

Because most students are inquirers who are curious and want to explore things around them, the science curriculum seeks to fuel this spirit of curiosity. The end goal is for students to enjoy science and value it as an important tool for exploring their natural and physical world. The teacher is a leader, facilitator and role model of the inquiry process in the science classroom and imparts the excitement and value of science to students by creating a learning environment that encourages and challenges students to develop a sense of inquiry (Ministry of Education, 2016c).

Science teachers are strongly encouraged to exercise professional judgement to develop a science curriculum and schemes of work that enhance the learning of science. Teachers incorporate ideas and materials from various sources based on the interests and abilities of students and they employ a variety of teaching and learning approaches for which the student is an inquirer (Ministry of Education, 2016c).

In Singapore schools, the traditional approach to conceptual teaching is replaced by more hands-on activities and science investigations. Also the current digital age has also made computer technology accessible in the classroom for improving science education. Based on the principles of the Integrated Curriculum Model (Van Tassel-Baska, 1986) that were developed for high-ability learners, the key elements of the classroom include accelerated content knowledge organised around main concepts, higher-order critical and creative thinking processes, curriculum differentiation and interdisciplinarity.

Because gifted students have self-directed learning skills which increase with age and correlate with their ability to think creatively (Torrance & Mourad, 1978), it is critical for teachers to create a student-centred classroom climate that encourages inquiry and independence. Self-directed learning allows increased student involvement and motivates them to learn (Treffinger, 1975), while collaboration promotes working with peers, mutual scaffolding, shared cognition and critical thinking as students engage as teams to solve challenging and complex learning tasks or problems (Diezmann & Watters, 2001).

Continuous formative assessment is useful for informing students of their progress and as an instructional tool for differentiating instruction for gifted students because they have diverse needs (Callahan, 2012). With the introduction of technology into the education scene, there is likely to be an improvement in students' digital literacy and confidence in using computers.

The curriculum in the school where our study took place specifically caters for intellectually-bright girls who are among the highest-scoring 3% of their cohort in the Primary School Leaving Examination. It provides a holistic, challenging and broad education that attempts to develop thinking skills and an appreciation for lifelong learning. The curriculum emphasises the cultivation of life skills such as resilience, teamwork, problem-solving and decision-making. In order to provide a stimulating classroom and to stretch students' minds, the school trains its teachers to deliver a science curriculum which emphasises higher-order thinking, self-directed learning, collaboration, curriculum differentiation, digital literacy and formative assessment.

RESEARCH METHODS

The purpose of this section is to describe the research methods employed in our comparative study of the effectiveness of using educational technology (namely, a one-student one-laptop program) among secondary science students in Singapore. Our pilot study is reported before providing specific details of our sample of 722 students and the two teaching methods (technology-based and regular instruction) that were compared. Because student attitudes were included as criteria of effectiveness in our evaluation, some widely-used science attitude instruments are considered before identifying, describing and justifying the four attitude scales that were selected for our research. Our study's criteria of instructional effectiveness also included characteristics of the classroom learning environment and therefore an overview of some past evaluations that involved assessing learning environment is provided, together with details about the six specific learning environment scales chosen for our research.

Pilot Study

Prior to using questionnaire scales in our main study, we conducted a pilot study, tried out data-collection techniques and estimated the time needed for students to respond. The appropriateness of questionnaire items also was assessed in terms of any misunderstandings, ambiguities or other inadequacies when administered in the population to be studied (Ary, Jacobs, Razavieh & Sorensen, 2006).

Our questionnaire was distributed to three teachers with a minimum of three years of experience with a request to identify any confusing items and to suggest changes in the wording to improve clarity and suitability for the school's formal language and cultural context. Based upon changes recommended by teachers, ten items were modified, taking care not to jeopardise face validity before field-testing items with students. A class of 33 students aged 13 to 14 years was chosen for the pilot study because students were similar to those in the main research. When the questionnaire was given to students, it took only approximately 8 minutes to respond to all the items.

Although the questionnaire was administered electronically in the main study, it was a deliberate decision to carry out the pilot study using a hard-copy questionnaire to facilitate interviews with students after completion of the questionnaire. Students were asked to revisit the items, circle those found to be ambiguous or confusing, and highlight any items for which their response was 'Not Sure'.

In the interview session, students were asked whether the instructions for responding to the questionnaire were clear. The purpose of the questionnaire was explained and any confusing items were re-worded. Students who had no problems with the clarity of items were asked to explain their interpretation. Students also proposed words and phrases that would allow items to be interpreted in a consistent manner and free from ambiguity. Further probing ensured common understanding, clarity and readability. Based on teachers' and students' feedback, two items were reworded.

Sample and Instructional Methods for Main Study

Student participants were high-ability learners among the top 1% to 3% scorers in Singapore's national examination for primary-school leavers. They attended a private school for high-ability learners in Singapore where the curriculum framework follows the Integrated Curriculum Model for the gifted by Van Tassel-Baska (1987). We received ethics approval from a university, as well as approval from the school principal.

The sample initially selected consisted of 777 students, with 409 grade 9 students in 14 technology-based science classes and 368 grade 10 students in 13 regular science classrooms. Respondents were aged from 14 to 16 years and were in self-contained classrooms with a class size of 30 to 35 students. Of the selected sample, 722 students consented to take part in the survey, which is almost 93% of the selected cohort. Complete and usable responses were obtained from 379 students in technology-based classrooms and 343 students in regular science classrooms.

After the purposes of the research and students' involvement were explained to students and their parents/legal guardians by means of a written letter, a written and signed consent form from parents/legal guardians was required prior to any student's participation. This was essential because all students in the sample were minors. Any student who did not receive written consent from her parent/legal guardian did not participate in the study. The letter indicated clearly that students' participation was voluntary and that they may discontinue their involvement at any time. The confidentiality of students' data was ensured and students' anonymity was guaranteed by coding all participants using numeric values to remove identifying features during data preparation and entry. Lastly, the letter advised parents that feedback on the progress of the study would be forthcoming in written form.

Technology-based classes comprised the pioneer cohort of students in a one-student one-laptop program. These students had been learning science for two and a half years while using laptops as learning tools. A typical lesson involved students accessing different types of media, including text, videos, images, models, simulations and animations. Students set their goals and targets and organised their learning using wikis, blogs, online calendars and email, accessed online libraries, databases and search engines to learn independently, collaborated with their peers both within their class synchronously or beyond class asynchronously, and created digital products using video-editing software, slideshows, animations and websites to demonstrate their learning. Science teachers provided lesson materials such as Powerpoint, Google Sheet and Google Docs using online platforms such as Edmodo and Google Domain, as well as conducting surveys and quizzes online to gather information about students' knowledge. During science practical lessons, students used electronic probes to collect data on light intensity, pH and humidity in order to share and compare real-time data with classmates or schoolmates. After lessons, students accessed teachers and experts without having to meet them face-to-face, submitted work online and received timely feedback from peers, teachers and experts.

On the other hand, in the regular science classes, students did not bring a laptop to school and they had been learning science during the last three and a half-years using hard-copy lesson materials such as textbooks, worksheets and notes. A typical lesson would involve the science teachers in using Powerpoint slides and internet sources such as videos and animation. Students did not have access to any online platforms, collaboration with peers was undertaken within class synchronously, and all student work was submitted as hard-copies. In summary, the type of curriculum and the experience of science teachers were similar in technology-based and regular classes, but the pedagogy employed was different.

Student Attitude Scales

Because our study included student attitudes as criteria in evaluating technology-based classrooms, this section provides a literature review about definitions of attitudes and questionnaires for assessing attitudes to science in past research. Thurstone (1928) was the first to claim that attitudes can be measured and defined attitude as "the sum total of a man's inclinations and feelings, prejudice and bias, preconceived notions, ideas, fears, threats and convictions about any specified topic" (p. 531). Attitudes are intangible psychological constructs that can be inferred from demonstrated actions (Eccles, 2007; Mueller, 1986) and are individually-attributed beliefs, emotions and behavioural tendencies (Baron & Byrne, 1977). Kerlinger (1986) defined an attitude as "...an organized predisposition to think, feel, perceive, and behave toward a referent or cognitive object" (p. 453). Reid (2006) delineated three components to attitudes: cognitive (knowledge of the object, belief or idea), affective (feelings regarding the object) and behavioural (the tendency towards action).

Many studies have shown that the number of students enrolled in science has declined over time (Bybee, 1994; Hilton et al., 1989; National Science, 1983; OECD, 2013; Osborne & Simon, 1996). Misiti, Shrigley and Hanson (1991) reported that the attitudes formed during middle-school years influence science subject choices in high school and college. Many past studies have reported that students only make science-related career choices if they develop a positive attitude towards science in school (Hofstein & Walberg, 1995; Lowe, 2004; Ormerod & Duckworth, 1975; Osborne & Simon, 1996). Gender equality in science enrolments and achievement continues to be a major problem (OECD, 2017).

In 1970, the first instrument to measure attitudes towards science, the Scientific Attitude Inventory (SAI), was designed by Moore and Sutman (1970) in the USA. The SAI assesses secondary-school students' knowledge of scientific laws and theories, as well as their feelings about being a scientist. For several years, the SAI was the main instrument used in over 30 studies throughout the world, but the validity of this instrument was in doubt (Munby, 1983). The SAI was revised by Moore and Fay (1997) to form the SAI II by gathering feedback and suggestions from researchers who had used it. The modified instrument was validated among 557 students in grades 6, 9 and 12. The improved version was shortened to 40 items, instead of the 60 items in the original SAI, and statements were re-worded to remove gender-biased language.

An instrument that has been used frequently to assess attitudes towards science is the Test of Science-Related Attitudes (TOSRA) (Fraser, 1978, 1981), which addresses potential problems with existing instruments such as demonstrated low reliability and construct validity, lack of clarity in the construct being assessed, and the invalid practice of combining conceptually-distinct constructs into one scale. TOSRA has 70 items (10 items in each of 7 scales), based on Klopfer's (1971) categories of attitudes in science education: Social Implications of Science, Normality of Scientists, Attitude to Scientific Inquiry, Adoption of Scientific Attitudes, Enjoyment of Science Lesson, Leisure Interest in Science, and Career Interest in Science. TOSRA was first field tested in Australia among 1,337 students in 44 classes from 11 different schools (Fraser, 1981). Later, several other studies confirmed its validity and reliability in Australia (Fraser et al., 2010; Fraser & Butts, 1982; Schibeci & McGaw, 1981), the United States (Lightburn & Fraser, 2007; Peiro & Fraser, 2009), Singapore (Peer & Fraser, 2015; Wong & Fraser, 1996) and Indonesia (Fraser et al., 2010). When Munby (1983) reviewed 56 science attitude instruments, he concluded that TOSRA is an exceptionally well-developed instrument.

The attitude scales used in our study were based on the Computer Attitudes Survey (CAS) and Students' Adaptive Learning Engagement in Science (SALES) questionnaire, which are discussed in detail below.

Attitudes to Computers Scale

The Attitudes to Computers scale used in our study was based on the Computer Attitudes Survey (CAS) which was designed originally by Loyd and Gressard (1984) and later modified by Newhouse (2001) to assess students' attitudes towards computers and computer programs. The original version of CAS containing 30 positively-worded and negatively-worded items was reported to be reliable and effective. Eight items were selected, adapted and used by Aldridge and Fraser (2008). This modified scale contains only positively-worded items that assess students' enjoyment or anxiety associated with using computers. We renamed this scale the Attitudes towards Computers scale and used it in our study because one of our objectives was to assess students' attitudes to using computers in either technology-based science classrooms or regular science classrooms.

Students' Adaptive Learning Engagement in Science (SALES) Questionnaire

The Students' Adaptive Learning Engagement in Science (SALES) questionnaire was designed to assess students' motivation and self-regulation in science learning (Velayutham, Aldridge & Fraser, 2011). 'Adaptive' describes characteristics that promote students' engagement in learning (Ames, 1992; Dweck, 1986; Kaplan & Maehr, 2007; Midgley, 2002; Pintrich, 2000). Motivation is a key dimension of attitudes (Tapia & Marsh, 2004) that leads to and focuses goal-oriented behaviour (Schunk, 2004).

Zimmerman (2002) identified three components of motivation associated with students' adaptive motivational beliefs – learning goal orientation, task value and self-efficacy – that are integral to successful engagement in self-regulated learning. The ability of students to self-regulate their learning is a central construct that influences students' engagement and achievement (Boekaerts & Cascallar, 2006). Both adaptive motivational beliefs and adaptive self-regulated learning foster student engagement in classroom activities (Pintrich, 2000).

We selected and used three of the SALES' four scales as being centrally relevant to our study: Task Value, Self-efficacy and Self-regulation. For each scale, there are 8 items with five frequency alternatives (Almost Never, Seldom, Sometimes, Often, and Almost Always). The SALES was originally validated with 1360 Grade 8 to 10 students in 78 classes from five different public schools in Australia (Velayutham et al., 2011) and subsequently cross-validated with 495 middle-school students in Florida, USA (Koren, 2013), 431 middle-school science students in South Australia (Rogers & Fraser, 2013), 1619 students in Afghanistan (Sayed, 2018) and 327 college students from the USA, the UAE and Turkey (Pasha-Zaida et al., in press).

Task Value, or the importance that students place on their assigned tasks (Velayutham et al., 2011) and it influences their attitudes towards science and science achievement (Tuan et al., 2005). Students who believe that their learning activities are important, interesting and useful and more likely to persevere in order to understand and finish tasks (Pintrich & De Groot, 1990; Wolters & Rosenthal, 2000). Even students with low self-efficacy can persist on tasks considered important (Schunk & Zimmerman 2007). The Task Value scale was selected for our study because we wanted to know whether students perceived science as relevant and whether there were differences between technology-based science classrooms and regular science classrooms for this attitude.

Self-efficacy is students' self-belief that they can achieve the desired outcomes and it is a strong predictor of student choices, effort and persistence (Velayutham et al., 2011). Having high self-efficacy in one subject does not guarantee high efficacy in another subject (Bandura, 1986, 1989; Pintrich & Schunk, 1995). Pajares (1996) claims that higher self-efficacy is associated with greater student willingness to persevere in challenging tasks and better academic performance. Self-efficacy has been found to be a stronger predictor of achievement and engagement in science than sex, ethnic background or parental background (Kupermintz, 2002). This scale was chosen for our study to identify any differences between technology-based science classrooms and regular science classrooms in students' belief in their own ability.

Self-regulation is the degree to which students are engaged in their learning and evaluate their progress (Velayutham et al., 2011). Boekaerts and Cascallar (2006) argue that students' self-regulation in classrooms is the most important influence on their engagement and achievement. The key aspect of self-regulation is students' use of cognitive and motivational strategies to achieve learning goals (Boekaerts & Cascallar, 2006). Zimmerman (2000) claims that motivation is a prerequisite for self-regulation.

Past studies have shown that higher self-regulation skills lead to academic motivation (Pintrich, 2003) and that short interventions for improving student self-regulation can lead to increased students' self-efficacy (Perels, Gurtler and Schmitz 2005). The self-regulation scale was chosen for our study because we wanted to identify differences between technology-based science classrooms and regular science classrooms in students' motivation to study science.

Learning Environment Criteria of Effectiveness

In selecting criteria of effectiveness for our study of technology-based instruction, we also drew on constructs and methods from the field of classroom learning environments (Fraser, 2012, 2014, 2018). Because one of the most common applications of learning environment instruments is as a source of criteria of effectiveness in evaluating educational programs or innovations, some of these past evaluations are reviewed below.

As well, another subsection below describes the six specific learning environment scales used in our study, namely, Investigation, Task Orientation, Collaboration, Differentiation, Computer Usage and Formative Assessment. Most of these scales are based on the Technology-Rich Outcomes-Focused Learning Environment Inventory (TROFLEI, Aldridge & Fraser, 2008).

Evaluation of Educational Innovations

In Singapore, researchers used classroom environment scales as dependent variables in evaluations of computer-assisted learning (Teh & Fraser, 1994), computer application courses for adults (Khoo & Fraser, 2008) and a pedagogical model known as the Mixed Mode Delivery (MMD) model (Koh & Fraser, 2014). When Maor and Fraser (1996) incorporated a classroom environment instrument in an evaluation of the use of a computerised database, students perceived more inquiry during the innovation. Nix et al. (2005) evaluated an innovative teacher development program (based on the Integrated Science Learning Environment, ISLE, model) in terms of the types of classroom learning environments fostered by teachers as perceived by their 445 students in 25 classes in Texas. Students whose teachers had attended the ISLE program perceived higher levels of Personal Relevance and Uncertainty of Science relative to comparison classes.

When Martin-Dunlop and Fraser (2008) evaluated an innovative science course for elementary-school teacher trainees in a university in California among 525 females in 27 classes, there were large difference (of over 1.5 standard deviations) between students' perceptions of the innovative course and their previous courses. Lightburn and Fraser (2007) used learning environment scales with 761 high-school biology students in 25 classes in Florida to assess the effectiveness of instruction involving anthropometry activities. The anthropometric group had higher scores on several scales relative to a comparison group.

In order to evaluate the effectiveness of an innovative new senior-high school in Western Australia in promoting outcomes-focused education, learning environment scales were used with a sample of 1918 students over a four-year period. Statistically-significant changes of moderate magnitude for seven scales over the four years supported the efficacy of the school's educational program (Aldridge & Fraser, 2008). Pickett and Fraser (2009) used learning environment scales to assess a two-year mentoring program in science for beginning teachers in an elementary school in southeastern USA. For a sample of seven beginning teachers and 573 elementary students, results supported the effectiveness of this mentoring program in improving the classroom learning environment, students' attitudes and achievement (Pickett & Fraser, 2009).

In New York, Wolf and Fraser (2008) evaluated the effectiveness of using inquiry-based laboratory activities in terms of learning environment, attitudes and achievement among 1,434 middle-school students in 71 science classes. Inquiry-based instruction promoted more student cohesiveness than non-inquiry instruction and inquiry-based instruction was differentially effective for male and female students. When Cohn and Fraser (2016) investigated the effectiveness of Student Response Systems (SRS) with 1097 students, the efficacy of SRS was supported. Oser and Fraser (2015) compared 322 grade 8–10 students' perceptions of the learning environment, attitudes towards science and achievement in virtual laboratories and physical laboratories. Although there were no significant differences between the two instructional groups, virtual laboratories were advantageous for males but disadvantageous for females on several criteria.

When Long and Fraser (2015) compared the learning environments of two middle-school science curriculum models (general science and a topic-specific) among 367 grade 8 students, the general curriculum model was more effective for Hispanic students but the two science models were equally effective for Caucasian students. When Afari et al. (2013) used classroom environment scales in the Arabic language with a sample of 352 college students from 33 classes in the United Arab Emirates, the use of mathematics games fostered a positive classroom environment.

Learning Environment Scales Used in Our Study

To assess classrooms that infuse technology into the curriculum and that focus on outcomes-based education, Aldridge et al. (2004) developed and validated the Technology-Rich Outcomes-Focused Learning Environment Inventory (TROFLEI), which is an extension of the commonly-used What Is Happening In this Class? (WIHIC) (Aldridge, Fraser & Huang, 1999). The TROFLEI includes all seven scales from the WIHIC (Student Cohesiveness, Teacher Support, Involvement, Investigation, Task Orientation, Cooperation and Equity) which was originally designed by Fraser et al. (1996), together with the three additional scales of Differentiation, Computer Usage and Young Adult Ethos. To identify if the teacher caters for individual differences, a Differentiation scale was adapted from the Individualised Classroom Environment Questionnaire (ICEQ; Fraser, 1990; Fraser & Butts, 1982). The extent and variety of ways in which computers are used in the classroom is assessed with the Computer Usage scale. A Young Adult Ethos scale was included to assess opportunities provided by teachers for self-directed learning. The TROFLEI is a suitable instrument to measure the learning experiences in gifted classrooms because the scales align with the instructional processes proposed to facilitate curriculum experiences for the gifted (Van Tassel-Baska & Stambaugh, 2006). For the purposes of our study, five of the TROFLEI's ten 8-item scales were included.

For a large sample of 2317 Australian students in 166 classes, Aldridge and Fraser (2008) reported strong factorial validity and internal consistency reliability for the TROFLEI. Aldridge, Dorman and Fraser (2004) used multitrait–multimethod modelling to validate the TROFLEI further with 1249 students from Tasmania and Western Australia. Welch, Cakir, Peterson and Ray (2012) cross-validated the TROFLEI with 980 grade 9–12 students from Turkey and 130 grade 9–12 students from the USA. In New Zealand, Koul, Fisher and Shaw (2011) cross-validated the TROFLEI with a sample of 1027 high-school students in 30 classes. In Florida, Earle and Fraser (2017) cross-validated the TROFLEI with 914 general-education students in 49 grade 6–8 mathematics classes.

Because all existing classroom environment questionnaires exclude scales related to the assessment of student learning, which are useful for informing learners of their progress, we chose one additional scale on assessment of student learning from the Constructivist-Orientated Learning Environment Survey (COLES) (Aldridge et al., 2012). COLES scales have been validated with 2034 grade 11 and 12 students in 147 classes across Western Australia (Aldridge et al., 2012).

Technology-Based Science Teaching among Gifted Females ... 51

Table 1. Instruments and scales chosen to assess student attitudes and learning environment

Desired Classroom Element[a]	Instrument	Scale	Description	Alpha Reliability
Student Attitudes				
Confidence in Using Computers	Attitudes towards Computers	CAS	The extent to which students have a positive attitude and confidence in using computers to perform learning tasks	0.90
Perceiving Science as Relevant	Task Value	SALES	The extent to which the student perceives the science learning tasks in terms of interest, importance and utility	0.88
Belief in One's Own Ability	Self-efficacy	SALES	The extent of the students' confidence and beliefs in their own ability in successfully perform science learning tasks	0.90
Motivation to Study Science	Self-regulation	SALES	The extent to which the students control and regulate their effort in science learning tasks	0.88
Learning Environment				
Higher-order Thinking	Investigation	TROFLEI	The extent to which students are given opportunities to evaluate problems, analyse generated ideas and synthesise information	0.87
Self-directed Learning	Task Orientation	TROFLEI	The extent to which the students perceive the importance of completing planned activities on their own and staying on the subject matter	0.86
Collaboration	Collaboration	TROFLEI	The extent to which students cooperate rather than compete with one another on learning tasks	0.87

Table 1. (Continued)

Desired Classroom Element[a]	Instrument	Scale	Description	Alpha Reliability
Differentiation	Differentiation	TROFLEI	The extent to which students perceive that teachers cater for students differently based on students' capabilities and interests	0.83
Digital Literacy	Computer Usage	TROFLEI	The extent to which students use their computers as a tool to communicate with others and to access information	0.84
Formative Assessment	Formative Assessment	COLES	The extent to which students feel that the assessment tasks given to them make a positive contribution to their learning	0.90

Adapted from CAS Computer Attitudes Survey (Newhouse, 2001), SALES, Student Adaptive Learning Engagement in Science (Velayutham et al. 2011), TROFLEI, Technology-Rich Outcomes-Focused Learning Environment Inventory (Aldridge and Fraser 2008) and COLES, Constructivist-Oriented Learning Environment Survey (Aldridge et al. 2012).
[a] Based on Van Tassell-Baska and Stambaugh (2006).

The school for high-ability learners in our study has a curriculum that emphasises higher-order thinking, self-directed learning, collaboration, differentiation, digital literacy and formative assessment. Therefore, for our study, we chose five scales from the TROFLEI and one scale on assessment of student learning from the COLES because these learning environment scales are aligned with the curriculum emphasis for the high-ability learners in the school.

Table 1 shows the 10 scales chosen to assess student attitudes and learning environment in our research, together with the instrument from which each scale was chosen and how these scales correspond with desired classroom elements recommended for gifted students (Van Tassel-Baska & Staumbaugh, 2006). As well, Table 1 provides scale descriptions and an estimate of each scale's reliability (using Cronbach's alpha coefficient) for our sample of 722 students. More-comprehensive validation analyses for this questionnaire (including factor analysis) is reported in Sundari (2017).

In our study, we retained the original positively-worded items because past studies have shown that this promotes response accuracy and internal consistency (Schriesheim, Eisenbach & Hill, 1991; Schriesheim & Hill, 1981). All 8 items in each scale were grouped together in a block rather than arranging them randomly or cyclically to provide contextual prompts, reduce confusion among students and ensure response assertiveness (Aldridge et al., 2000).

RESULTS: DIFFERENCES BETWEEN TECHNOLOGY-BASED AND REGULAR CLASSROOMS IN STUDENTS' ATTITUDES AND THE LEARNING ENVIRONMENT

In this section, differences between our technology-based science classrooms and regular science classrooms, with regards to students' attitudes and perceptions of classroom learning environment, are reported. The statistical significance of differences between technology-based and regular classrooms in terms of student attitudes and learning environment was investigated with multivariate analysis of variance (MANOVA). The instructional method (technology-based vs regular classes) was the independent variable whereas the 4 attitude scales and 6 learning environment scales were the dependent variables. When the multivariate test using Wilks' lambda criterion revealed statistically-significant differences between the two instructional methods for the dependent variables as a whole, univariate ANOVA results for each individual dependent variable were interpreted separately and recorded in Table 2. Initially conducting MANOVA provided protection against Type 1 errors.

Table 2. Average item mean, average item standard deviation and difference between technology-based and regular science classes (ANOVA result and effect size) for each attitude and learning environment scale

Scale	Item Mean		Item SD		Difference	
	Technology-based	Regular	Technology-based	Regular	F	Effect Size (Cohen's d)
Student Attitudes						
Attitudes to Computers	3.32	3.03	0.77	0.79	26.11**	0.37
Task Value	3.96	3.93	0.55	0.54	0.38	0.06
Self-Efficacy	3.47	3.40	0.66	0.66	2.25	0.11
Self-Regulation	3.92	3.75	0.53	0.64	15.60**	0.31
Learning Environment						
Investigation	3.34	3.10	0.67	0.67	22.94**	0.36
Task Orientation	4.14	3.92	0.56	0.55	28.84**	0.40
Collaboration	4.13	4.01	0.56	0.55	8.24**	0.22
Differentiation	2.32	2.23	0.78	0.70	2.62	0.12
Computer Usage	3.36	2.64	0.58	0.73	217.56**	1.09
Formative Assessment	4.02	3.89	0.58	0.66	8.24**	0.27

**$p<0.01$ N=722 in 27 classes.
Cohen's d is calculated by dividing the difference between the means by the root mean square of the two standard deviations.

Differences between the two instructional methods were statistically significant for seven scales. Table 2 shows that students in technology-based science classrooms had higher scores for Attitudes to Computers, Self-Regulation, Investigation, Task Orientation, Collaboration, Computer Usage and Formative Assessment than students in regular science classrooms. Differences between technology-based and regular science instruction were not statistically significant for Differentiation, Task Value and Self-Efficacy.

Regarding differences between technology-based and regular science classes, effect sizes were calculated to provide measures of the magnitudes of observed differences (Field, 2009) that are independent of sample size. Cohen's d was calculated by dividing the difference between means by the pooled standard deviation (Cohen, 1988). According to Cohen (1992), an effect size of less than 0.20 can be considered small, of 0.5 is moderate and of 0.80 or greater is a large effect size. See Table 2 for the effect sizes for differences between technology-based and regular science instruction for each attitude and learning environment scale.

For those scales for which differences between technology-based and regular classes were statistically significant (Attitudes to Computers, Self-regulation, Investigation, Task Orientation, Collaboration, Computer Usage and Formative Assessment), effect sizes were 0.37, 0.31, 0.36, 0.40, 0.22, 1.09 and 0.27, standard deviations, respectively. Based on Cohen's criteria, these effect sizes are small/moderate for all scales except for Computer Usage for which the effect size is large. Overall, the results reported in Table 2 support the effectiveness of this technology-based instructional method (one-student one-laptop) for gifted science students in Singapore.

CONCLUSION

This chapter has provided a review of the history of gifted education, the approach to gifted education specifically in Singapore, the Singaporean educational context, and the science curriculum for the gifted in Singapore. Also this chapter has reported a comparative evaluation of the effectiveness of technology-based science instruction for a sample of 722 secondary-school learners using students' attitudes and perceptions of their classroom environments as criteria.

A comparison of technology-based and regular science classrooms revealed statistically-significant differences in favour of technology-based instruction for the seven scales of Attitudes to Computers, Self-regulation, Investigation, Task Orientation, Collaboration, Computer Usage and Formative Assessment. For these scales, the effect sizes for the differences between instructional groups were of modest magnitudes for six scales, ranging from 0.22 to 0.40 standard deviations. However, the effect size was large for the Computer Usage scale and exceeded 1.0 standard deviations. Overall, our study supported the effectiveness of this one-student one-laptop program for gifted science learners.

REFERENCES

Afari, E., Aldridge, J. M., Fraser, B. J., & Khine, M. S. (2013). Students' perception of the learning environment and attitudes in game-based mathematics classrooms. *Learning Environments Research, 16*, 131-150.

Aldridge, J. M., Dorman, J. P., & Fraser, B. J. (2004). Use of multi-trait–multi-method modelling to validate actual and preferred forms of the Technology-Rich Outcomes-Focused Learning Inventory (TROFLEI). *Australian Journal of Educational and Developmental Psychology, 4*, 110-125.

Aldridge, J. M., & Fraser, B. J. (2008). *Outcomes-focused learning environments: Determinants and effects*. Rotterdam, The Netherlands: Sense Publishers.

Aldridge, J. M., Fraser, B. J., Bell, L., & Dorman, J. (2012). Using a new learning environment questionnaire for reflection in teacher action research. *Journal of Science Teacher Education, 23*(3), 259-290.

Aldridge, J. M., Fraser, B. J., & Huang, I. T. C. (1999). Investigating classroom environments in Taiwan and Australia with multiple research methods. *Journal of Educational Research, 93*, 48-62.

Aldridge, J. M., Fraser, B. J., Taylor, P. C., & Chen, C. C. (2000). Constructivist learning environments in a cross-national study in Taiwan and Australia. *International Journal of Science Education, 22*, 37-55.

Ames, C. (1992). Classrooms: Goals, structures, and student motivation. *Journal of Educational Psychology, 84*, 261-271.

Ary, D., Jacobs, L. C., Razavieh, A., & Sorensen, C. (2006). *Introduction to research in education* (7th ed.). Belmont, CA: Thomson Wadsworth.

Bandura, A. (1986). *Social foundations of thought and action: A social cognitive theory*. Englewood Cliffs, NJ: Prentice Hall.

Bandura, A. (1989). Human agency in social cognitive theory. *American Psychologist, 44*, 1175-1184.

Baron, R. A., & Byrne, D. E. (1977). *Social psychology: Understanding human interaction*. Boston: Allyn and Bacon.

Bernreuter, R. G., Miles, C. C., Tinker, M. A., & Young, K. (1942). *Studies in personality*. New York: McGraw-Hill Book Company.

Binet, A., & Simon, T. (1905). Méthodes nouvelles pour le diagnostic du niveaux [New methods for diagnosing abnormal intellectual levels]. *L'année Psychologique, 11*, 191–336.

Boekaerts, M., & Cascallar, E. (2006). How far have we moved toward the integration of theory and practice in self-regulation? *Educational Psychology Review, 18*, 199-210.

Boring, E. G. (1950). *A history of experimental psychology*. Upper Saddle River, NJ: Prentice Hall.

Burg, B. (1992). Gifted education in Israel. *Roeper Review, 14*, 217-221.

Bybee, R. W. (1994). *Reforming science education: Social perspectives and personal reflections*. New York: Teachers College Press.

Cakir, M. (2011). Validity and reliability of the Turkish form of Technology-Rich Outcome-Focused Learning Environment Inventory. *Kuram Uygulamada Egit. Bilim, 11*(4), 1959-1963.

Callahan, C. M. (2012). *Fundamentals of gifted education: Considering multiple perspectives*. Hoboken: Taylor and Francis.

Cohen, J. (1988). *Statistical power analysis for the behavioral sciences* (2nd ed.). Hillsdale, NJ: Lawrence Erlbaum.

Cohen, J. (1992). A power primer. *Psychological Bulletin, 112*, 155-159.

Colangelo, N., & Davis, G. A. (2003). *Handbook of gifted education* (3rd ed.). Boston: Allyn & Bacon.

Davis, G. A., & Rimm, S. B. (2004). *Education of the gifted and talented*. Boston: Pearson Education.

Diezmann, C. M., & Watters, J. J. (2001). The collaboration of mathematically gifted students on challenging tasks. *Journal for the Education of the Gifted, 25*(1), 7-31.

Dweck, C. S. (1986). Motivational process affecting learning. *American Psychologist, 41*, 1040-1048.

Earle, J. E., & Fraser, B. J. (2017). Evaluating online resources in terms of classroom environment and student attitudes in middle-grade mathematics. *Learning Environments Research, 20*, 339-364.

Eccles, L. (2007). *Gender differences in teacher-student interactions, attitudes and achievement in middle school science* (Unpublished PhD thesis, Curtin University).

Fraser, B. J. (1978). Development of a test of science-related attitudes. *Science Education, 62*, 509-515.

Fraser, B. J. (1981). *Test of Science Related Attitudes (TOSRA)*. Melbourne, Australia: Australian Council for Educational Research.

Fraser, B. J. (1990). *Individualised Classroom Environment Questionnaire*. Melbourne, Australia: Australian Council for Educational Research.

Fraser, B. J. (2012). Classroom learning environments: Retrospect, context and prospect. In B. J. Fraser, K. G. Tobin, C.J. McRobbie (Eds.), *The second international handbook for science education research* (pp. 1191-1239). New York: Springer.

Fraser, B. J. (2014). Classroom learning environments: Historical and contemporary perspectives. In N. G. Lederman & S. K. Abell (Eds.), *Handbook of research on science education volume II* (pp. 104-119). New York: Routledge.

Fraser, B. J. (2018). Milestones in the evolution of the learning environments field over the past three decades. In D. B. Zandvliet and B. J. Fraser (Eds.), *Thirty years of learning environments research: Looking back and looking forward* (pp. 1-19). Leiden, the Netherlands: Brill | Sense.

Fraser, B. J., Aldridge, J. M., & Adolphe, F. S. G. (2010). A cross-national study of secondary science classroom environments in Australia and Indonesia. *Research in Science Education, 40*, 551-571.

Fraser, B. J., & Butts, W. L. (1982). Relationship between perceived levels of classroom individualization and science-related attitudes. *Journal of Research in Science Teaching, 19*, 143-154.

Fraser, B. J., Fisher, D. L., & McRobbie, C. J. (1996, April). *Development, validation, and use of personal and class forms of a new classroom environment instrument*. Paper presented at the presented at the annual meeting of the American Educational Research Association, New York.

Gross, M. (1999). Inequity in equity: The paradox of gifted education in Australia. *Australian Journal of Education, 43*(1), 87-103.

Hilton, T. L., Hsia, J., Solorzano, D. G., & Benton, N. L. (1989). *Persistence in science of high-ability minority students*. Princeton, NJ: Educational Testing Service.

Hofstein, A., & Walberg, H. J. (1995). Instructional strategies. In B. J. Fraser & H. J. Walberg (Eds.), *Improving science education* (pp. 1-20). Chicago, IL: National Society for the Study of Education.

Hollingworth, L. S. (Ed.). (1940). *Intelligence* as an element of personality. In G. M. Whipple (Ed.), *Intelligence: Its nature and nurture: Part I. Comparative and critical exposition* (39th Yearbook of National Society for the Study of Education). Bloomington, IL: Public School Publishing.

Kaplan, A., & Maehr, M. L. (2007). The contribution and prospects of goal orientation theory. *Educational Psychology Review, 19*, 141-187.

Kerlinger, F. N. (1986). *Foundations of behavioral research* (3rd ed.). Fort Worth, TX: Holt, Rinehart, and Winston.

Klopfer, L. E. (1971). Evaluation of learning in science. In B. S. Bloom, J. T. Hastings, & G. F. Madaus (Eds.), *Handbook on summative and formative evaluation of student learning* (pp. 559-642). New York: McGraw-Hill.

Koh, N. K., & Fraser, B. J. (2014). Learning environment associated with use of mixed mode delivery model among secondary business studies students in SIngapore. *Learning Environments Research, 17*(2), 157-171.

Koren, J. A. (2013). *A comparative study of gifted and non-gifted middle-school students in terms of classroom environment and attitudes within a large urban school district* (Unpublished PhD thesis, Curtin University).

Koul, R. B., Fisher, D. L., & Shaw, T. (2011). An application of the TROFLEI in secondary-school science classes in New Zealand. *Research in Science and Technological Education, 29*(2), 147-167.

Kupermintz, H. (2002). Affective and cognitive factors as aptitude resources in high school science achievement. *Educational Assessment, 8*, 123-137.

Lightburn, M. E., & Fraser, B. J. (2007). Classroom environment and student outcomes among students using anthropometry activities in high school science. *Research in Science and Technological Education, 25*, 153-166.

Lockwood, A. (1992a). The de facto curriculum? *Focus in Change, 6*, 8-11.

Lockwood, A. (1992b). Whose knowledge do we teach? *Focus in Change, 6*, 3-7.

Long, C., & Fraser, B. J. (2015). Comparison of alternative sequencing of middle-school science curriculum: Classroom learning environment and student attitudes. *Curriculum and Teaching, 30*(1), 23-36.

Lowe, J. P. (2004). *The effect of cooperative group work and assessment on the attitudes of students towards science in New Zealand* (Unpublished PhD thesis, Curtin University).

Loyd, B. D., & Gressard, C. (1984). Reliability and factorial validity of computer attitudes scales. *Educational and Psychological Measurement, 44*, 501-505.

Maor, D., & Fraser, B. J. (1996). Use of classroom environment perceptions in evaluating inquiry-based computer assisted learning. *International Journal of Science Education, 18*, 401-421.

Martin-Dunlop, C., & Fraser, B. J. (2008). Learning environment and attitudes associated with an innovative course designed for prospective elementary teachers. *International Journal of Science and Mathematics Education, 6*, 163-190.

Midgley, C. (2002). *Goals, goal structures, and patterns of adaptive learning.* Mahwah. NJ: Lawrence Erlbaum.

Ministry of Education, Singapore. (2016a). *Education System*. Retrieved August 8, 2016, from https://www.moe.gov.sg/education/education-system.

Ministry of Education, Singapore. (2016b). *Gifted Education Programme*. Retrieved August 5, 2016, from https://www.moe.gov.sg/education/programmes/gifted-education-programme/rationale-and-goals.

Ministry of Education, Singapore. (2016c). *Sciences*. Retrieved August 5, 2016, from https://www.moe.gov.sg/education/syllabuses/sciences/.

Misiti, F. L., Shrigley, R. L., & Hanson, L. (1991). Science attitude scale for middle school students. *Science Education, 75*, 525-540.

Moore, R. W., & Foy, R. L. (1997). The Scientific Attitude Inventory: A revision (SAI II). *Journal of Research in Science Teaching, 34*, 327-336.

Moore, R. W., & Sutman, F. X. (1970). The development, field test and validation of an inventory of scientific attitude. *Journal of Research in Science Teaching, 7*, 85-94.

Mueller, D. J. (1986). *Measuring social attitudes. A handbook for researchers and practitioners*. New York: Teacher College Press.

Munby, H. (1983). Thirty studies involving the "Scientific Attitude Inventory": What confidence can we have in this instrument? *Journal of Research in Science Teaching, 20*, 141-162.

National Association for Gifted Children. (2008). *A brief history of gifted and talented education*. Retrieved June 6, 2015, from http://www.nagc.org/resources-publications/resources/gifted-education-us/brief-history-gifted-and-talented-education

National Library Board, Singapore. (2015). *Gifted Education Programme is introduced*. Retrieved June 8, 2015, from http://eresources.nlb.gov.sg/history/events/74f49f3c-3536-4ef0-8d33-8e985275fb85.

National Library Board, Singapore. (2016). *New Education System is introduced*. Retrieved August 5, 2016 from http://eresources.nlb.gov.sg/history/events /832f0610-d78c-4560-a2d5-b72c2858ce1a.

National Science Board Commission on Precollege Education in Mathematics, Science, and Technology. (1983). *Educating Americans for the 21st century*. Washington, DC: National Science Foundation.

Newhouse, C. P. (2001). Development and use of an instrument for computer-supported learning environments. *Learning Environments Research, 4*, 115-138.

Nix, R. K., Fraser, B. J., & Ledbetter, C. E. (2005). Evaluating an integrated science learning environment using the Constructivist Learning Environment Survey. *Learning Environments Research, 8*, 109-133.

OECD (Organisation for Economic Cooperation and Development). (2013). *Education at a glance 2013: OECD indicators.* Paris: OECD.

OECD (Organisation for Economic Cooperation and Development). (2017). *The pursuit of gender equality: An uphill battle.* Paris: OECD.

Ormerod, M. B., & Duckworth, D. (1975). *Pupils' attitudes to science.* Slough, England: National Foundation for Educational Research.

Osborne, J., & Simon, S. (1996). Primary science: Past and future directions. *Studies in Science Education, 27*(1), 99-147.

Pajares, F. (1996). Self-efficacy during childhood and adolescence: Implications for teachers and parents. In F. Pajares & T. Urdan (Eds.), *Adolescence and education: Self-efficacy beliefs of adolescents* (pp. 339-367). Greenwich, CT: Information Age Publishing.

Pasha-Zaidi, N., Afari, E., Sevi, B., Urganci, B., & Durham, J. (in press). Responsibility of learning: A cross-cultural examination of the relationship of grit, motivational beliefs and self-regulation among college students in the US, UAE and Turkey. *Learning Environments Research.* https://doi.org/10.1007/s10984-018-9268-y.

Peer, J., & Fraser, B. J. (2015). Sex, grade-level and stream differences in learning environment and attitudes to science in Singapore primary schools. *Learning Environments Research, 18*(1), 143-161.

Peiro, M. M., & Fraser, B. J. (2009). Assessment and investigation of science learning environments in the early childhood grades. In M. Ortiz & C. Rubio (Eds.), *Educational evaluation: 21st century issues and challenges* (pp. 349-365). New York: Nova Science Publishers.

Perels, F., Gurtler, T., & Schmitz, B. (2005). Training of self-regulatory and problem-solving competence. *Learning and Instruction, 15*, 123-139.

Pickett, L. H., & Fraser, B. J. (2009). Evaluation of a mentoring programme for beginning teachers in terms of the learning environment and student outcomes in participants' school classrooms. In A. Selkirk & M. Tichenor (Eds.), *Teacher education: Policy, practice and research* (pp. 1-52). New York: Nova Science Publishers.

Pintrich, P. R. (2000). The role of goal orientation in self-regulated learning. In P. R. Pintrich & M. Zeidner (Eds.), *Handbook of self-regulation* (pp. 451-502). San Diego, CA: Academic.

Pintrich, P. R. (2003). A motivational science perspective on the role of student motivation in learning and teaching contexts. *Journal of Educational Psychology, 95*, 667-686.

Pintrich, P. R., & De Groot, E. V. (1990). Motivational and self-regulated learning components of classroom academic performance. *Journal of Educational Psychology, 82*, 33-40.

Pintrich, P. R., & Schunk, D. H. (1995). *Motivation in education: Theory, research, and applications*. Englewood Cliffs, NJ: Prentice Hall.

Quek, C. G. (1997). *An overview of the Singapore Gifted Education Programme (GEP)*. Paper presented at the 1st International Conference on Special Education, Brunei Darussalam.

Reid, N. (2006). Thoughts on attitude measurement. *Research in Science and Technological Education, 24*, 3-27.

Rogers, J., & Fraser, B.J. (2013 April). *Sex and frequency of practical work as determinants of middle-school science students' attitudes and aspirations.* Paper presented at the annual meeting of the American Educational Research Association, San Francisco.

Sattler, J. M. (1992). *Assessment of children: Revised and updated* (3rd ed.). San Diego, CA: Jerome M. Sattler, Publisher, Inc.

Sayed, A. (2018). *Science classroom learning environments in Afghanistan: Assessment, effects and determinants*. (Unpublished PhD thesis, Curtin University).

Schibeci, R. A., & McGaw, B. (1981). Empirical validation of the conceptual structure of a test of science related attitudes. *Educational & Psychological Measurement, 41*, 1195-1201.

Schriesheim, C. A., Eisenbach, R. J., & Hill, K. D. (1991). The effect of negation and polar opposite item reversals on questionnaire reliability and validity: An experimental investigation. *Educational and Psychological Measurement, 51*(1), 67-78.

Schriesheim, C. A., & Hill, K. D. (1981). Controlling acquiescence response bias by item reversals: The effect on questionnaire validity. *Educational and Psychological Measurement, 41*(4), 1101-1114.

Schunk, D. H. (2004). *Learning theories: An educational perspective.* Upper Saddle River, NJ: Pearson Prentice Hall.

Schunk, D. H., & Zimmerman, B. J. (2007). Influencing children's self-efficacy and self-regulation of reading and writing through modeling. *Reading & Writing Quarterly, 23*, 7-25.

Silverman, L. K. (2013). *Giftedness 101.* New York: Springer.

Sundari, G. (2017). *Gifted females' attitudes and perceptions of learning environment in technology-based science classrooms in Singapore.* (Unpublished PhD thesis, Curtin University).

Tapia, M., & Marsh, G. (2004). An instrument to measure mathematics attitudes. *Academic Exchange Quarterly, 8*(2), 1-8.

Teh, G. P. L., & Fraser, B. J. (1994). An evaluation of computer-assisted learning in terms of achievement, attitudes and classroom environment. *Evaluation & Research in Education, 8*(3), 147-159.

Teh, G. P. L., & Fraser, B. J. (1995). Development and validation of an instrument for assessing the psychosocial environment of computer-assisted learning classrooms. *Journal of Educational Computing Research, 12,* 177-193.

Terman, L. M. (1925). *Mental and physical traits of a thousand gifted children: Genetic studies of genius* (Vol. 1). Stanford, CA: Stanford University Press.

Thurstone, L. L. (1928). Attitudes can be measured. *American Journal of Sociology, 33*, 529-544.

Torrance, E. P., & Mourad, S. (1978). Some creativity and style of learning and thinking correlates of Guglielmino's Self-directed Readiness Scale. *Psychological Reports, 43*, 1167-1171.

Treffinger, D. J. (1975). Teaching for self-directed learning: A priority for the gifted and talented. *Gifted Child Quarterly, 29*, 46-59.

Van Tassel-Baska, J. (1986). Acceleration. In J. Maker (Ed.), *Critical issues in gifted education* (pp. 179-186). Rockville, MD: Aspen.

Van Tassel-Baska, J. (1987). The ineffectiveness of the pull-out programme model in gifted education: A minority perspective. *Journal of Education of the Gifted, 10*(4), 255-264.

Van Tassel-Baska, J. (2003). What matters in curriculum for gifted learners: Reflection on theory, research and practice. In N. Colangelo & G.A. Davis (Eds.), *Handbook of gifted education* (3rd ed., pp. 174-183). Boston: Allyn & Bacon.

Van Tassel-Baska, J., Bass, G., Reis, R., Poland, D., & Avery L.D. (1998). A national study of science curriculum effectiveness with high ability students. *Gifted Child Quarterly, 42 (4)*, 200-211.

Van Tassel-Baska, J., & Stambaugh, T. (2006). *Comprehensive curriculum for gifted learners*. Boston: Pearson Education, Inc.

Velayutham, S., Aldridge, J. M., & Fraser, B. J. (2011). Development and validation of an instrument to measure students' motivation and self-regulation in science learning. *International Journal of Science Education, 33*(15), 2159-2179.

Welch, A. G., Cakir, M., Peterson, C. M., & Ray, C. M. (2012). A cross-cultural validation of the Technology-Rich Outcomes-Focused Learning Environment Inventory (TROFLEI) in Turkey and the USA. *Research in Science and Technological Education, 30*(1), 49-63.

Wechsler, D. (1949). *Wechsler intelligence scale for children*. San Antonio, TX: The Psychological Corporation.

Wolf, S. J., & Fraser, B. J. (2008). Learning environment, attitudes and achievement among middle-school science students using inquiry-based laboratory activities. *Research in Science Education, 38*, 321-341.

Wolters, C. A., & Rosenthal, H. (2000). The relation between students' motivational beliefs and their use of motivational regulation strategies. *International Journal of Educational Research, 33*, 801-820.

Wong, A. L. F., & Fraser, B. J. (1996). Environment-attitudes associations in the chemistry laboratory classroom. *Research in Science and Technological Education, 14*, 91-102.

Yurkevich, V. S., & Davidovich, B. M. (2009). Russian strategies for talent development: Stimulating comfort and discomfort. In T. Balchin, Hymer, B. & Matthews, D. J. (Eds.), *The Routledge international companion to gifted education* (pp. 101-105). New York: Routledge.

Zenderland, L. (1998). *Measuring minds: Henry Herbert Goddard and the origins of American intelligence testing*. Cambridge: Cambridge University Press.

Zimmerman, B. J. (2000). Self-efficacy: An essential motive to learn. *Contemporary Educational Psychology, 25*, 82-91.

Zimmerman, B. J. (2002). Becoming a self-regulated learner: An overview. *Theory into Practice, 41*, 64-70.

In: Science Teaching and Learning
Editor: Paul J. Hendricks

ISBN: 978-1-53617-406-9
© 2020 Nova Science Publishers, Inc.

Chapter 3

THE PROBLEM OF PERCEPTION: CHALLENGING STUDENTS' VIEWS OF SCIENCE AND SCIENTISTS THROUGH SCHOOL-SCIENTIST PARTNERSHIPS

*Garry Falloon**

The School of Education, The Faculty of Arts,
Macquarie University, North Ryde, Sydney, Australia

ABSTRACT

More than 50 years ago, Margaret Mead and Rhoda Metráux surveyed 35,000 students to explore their views of science and scientists. Their study revealed that students held very different *personal* to *public* views, and that despite acknowledging the importance of science, attitudes towards personal engagement in science or with scientists, was generally negative. Later work by researchers such as Chambers (1983), Finson, Beaver and Cramond (1995), and Finson (2002) confirmed this to be an enduring issue, as revealed through studies using instruments such as the *Draw a Scientist Test (DAST)* and the *Draw a Scientist Test Checklist (DAST-C)*. However, some researchers concerned with this

---

* Corresponding Author's Email: garry.falloon@mq.edu.au.

issue point to the possible value of scientists working with teachers in school-scientist partnerships (SSPs) as means of addressing some of these negative views. This chapter reports methods and outcomes from a study that explored the impact of a six-month SSP involving a New Zealand science research institute and a group of 164, 9-10 year olds. It used the DAST-C, a short response questionnaire and semi-structured interviews, to investigate the influence of the partnership on students' views of science and scientists. Results suggest the partnership had some positive impact on students' existing stereotypical views that could be attributed to specific design features, but that other aspects of the partnership, such as how it was executed in the classroom, actually appeared to *reinforce* negative perceptions. Recommendations are made that it is hoped will provide guidance for designing and implementing similar initiatives.

Keywords: scientists, perception, stereotype, partnership, engagement, science

INTRODUCTION

Over a number of years, significant research has been completed exploring students' views of science and scientists, and speculating how this may impact in areas such as career choice, the selection of higher level science study, and engagement in and views of science generally (e.g., Balcin & Ergün, 2018; Boylan, Hill, Wallace & Wheeler, 1992; Chambers, 1983; Finson, 2002; Huber & Burton, 1995; McCarthy, 2015; Shin et al., 2015; Thomson, Zakaria & Radut-Taciu, 2019). Much of this has been in response to calls from governments, industries, and scientific agencies for improved levels of STEM (Science, Technology, Engineering and Mathematics) capability derived from education systems, and enhanced STEM literacy in the general population. While some recent studies (e.g., Hillman, Bloodsworth, Tilburg, Zeeman & List, 2014), point to possible improvements in students' views of science and scientists from the stereotyped and generally negative perceptions revealed in earlier work (e.g., Chambers, 1983; Mead & Metráux, 1957), other studies challenge this conclusion (e.g., Avraamidou, 2013; Thomson et al., 2019).

The Problem of Perception

In an effort to address enduring negative perceptions of science and scientists held by many young people, researchers and teachers have designed and implemented specific interventions focused on challenging existing stereotypes of scientists as "male individuals wearing a gown, glasses or protective glasses, tie or bow tie, moustache and with a peculiar hairstyle or no hair (surrounded by laboratory equipment)" (Balcin & Ergün, 2018, p. 66). Initiatives include curriculum designed to expose students to alternative models of science (Shin et al., 2015), providing improved access to pre-course science experiences (Milford & Tippett, 2013), implementing STEM-fellow programs (Hillman et al., 2014) and incorporating science history and out of class science experiences in courses (McCarthy, 2015). Recently, research attention has turned to exploring the efficacy of school-scientist or scientist-teacher-student (STS) partnerships as a means of challenging students' perceptions. In these, practicing scientists from universities or research institutes work alongside classroom teachers in collaborative programs designed to enrich students' science learning, through combining pedagogical and science knowledge and expertise in relevant and authentic educational experiences. Partnerships vary in nature but typically comprise interactions lasting for several weeks, offering potential advantages over more traditional models that Shin et al. (2015) describe as "often short-term (such as) visits to a scientist's lab or short, isolated visits by a scientist to an elementary school classroom" (p. 3). Shin et al. (2015) comments that while true partnerships can be challenging and time-consuming to establish, they offer significant potential for "providing students with access to career role models... that support the development of student career aspirations through the cultivation of positive perceptions of science and scientists" (p. 10). This conclusion is also supported by the earlier work of Falloon (2013), Falloon and Trewern (2009), and Peker and Dolan (2012).

However, while partnerships in their various forms are becoming increasingly common, relatively few studies have employed tools to determine the influence of these longer interventions on students' views of science and the work of scientists (Painter, Jones, Tretter & Kubasco, 2010). Those that have been undertaken have usually investigated shorter-term programs, such as volunteer 'visiting scientist' schemes (Tuschi, 2008), STEM-fellowships (Hillman et al., 2014), or scientists working with teachers to develop curriculum materials (Brown, Bokor, Crippen & Koroly, 2014). This study used the Draw-a-Scientist Checklist (DAST-C; Finson et al., 1995), a short response questionnaire, and semi-structured interviews to explore the impact of a six-month SSP on the views of science and scientists held by 164 year five and six students (9-10 year olds) in a provincial New Zealand primary school. It profiles before and after partnership perceptions, and discusses possible reasons for changes linked to specific aspects of the partnership. It also identifies limitations in the DAST-C, highlighting the importance of using multiple measures to gain accurate insights into the real meaning behind students' representations.

STUDENTS' VIEWS OF SCIENCE AND SCIENTISTS

Very early work to better understand students' views of science and scientists undertaken by Mead and Metráux (1957) on behalf of the American Association for the Advancement of Science, surveyed nearly 35,000 high school students in 120 schools, using an exercise where students were required to respond to short statements about how they perceived science and scientists. Their findings indicated that students held considerably different *public* to *personal* views. That is, while students publicly valued and appreciated science as an endeavour (responsible for progress, improving quality of life, providing medical and health benefits etc.); when it came to actually being involved personally in a science career or associated with someone involved in science (e.g., a close relative), views were generally negative. Building on Mead and Metráux's (1957) study, later research has concentrated on trying to discover the reasons for students' poor personal views "hoping to gain understanding of students' negative attitudes about science, and in particular, about becoming a scientist" (Kahle, 1989, p. 3).

The historical pattern of *entrenchment* of stereotyped images of scientists as students work their way through education systems, has been confirmed in many studies (Huber & Burton, 1995; Jones, Howe & Rua, 2000; Moseley & Norris, 1999; Reap, Cavallo & McWhirter, 1994; Rosenthal, 1993; Sumrall, 1995; Thomas, Pedersen & Finson, 2001). While some more recent work has identified an improvement in this situation (Hillman et al., 2014; Miele, 2014; Milford & Tippet, 2013), according to others "scientists are (still) typically portrayed as male, with lab coats, conducting dangerous experiments in the lab" (Fralick, Kearn, Thompson & Lyons, 2009, p. 66). While some difference in results can be attributed to variation in methodological approaches, the early emergence and enduring nature of stereotypical views of scientists is well reported in literature (Eugster, 2013), and has been linked by some to representations in popular media (Painter et al., 2006; Tan, Jocz & Zhai, 2017) and a lack of student understanding of the 'real world' work of scientists (Shin et al., 2015). This enduring issue is concerning, given the need to raise levels of STEM literacy and engagement both in schools and in societies generally. School-scientist partnerships (SSPs) have been promoted as effective for exposing students and teachers to more accurate information about scientists' work, challenging stereotypes, and assisting to form correct understandings of the nature and value of scientific endeavour.

SCHOOL-SCIENTIST PARTNERSHIPS (SSPs)

School-scientist partnerships (SSPs) are not new, becoming popular in the United States in the 1980s in response to government calls for private sector science and technology-based enterprises to partner with schools to improve the ailing state of science education. Brown et al. (2014) describe school-scientist partnerships as "a unique form of professional development, that can assist teachers in translating current science into classroom instruction by involving them in meaningful collaborations with university researchers (and scientists)" (p. 239). Tanner, Chatman and Allen (2013) add that SSPs have the ultimate goal of "improving science education along the kindergarten through postgraduate education continuum" (p. 240), and that they rely on professional recognition, collaboration, collective participation, bi-directional flow of information, and instructional alignment with curriculum and students' learning needs, to be successful. However, despite their long history, according to Painter, Thomas, Jones and Kubasko "few studies have attempted to establish the impact of collaborations between scientific and science education communities" (2006, p. 183). They further comment that those that have "reported only anecdotal evidence for the influence of scientists in the classroom" (2006, p. 183).

However, one partnership reporting significant student benefits was the *Partnership for Research and Education in Plants* (PREP) project (Peker & Dolan, 2012). This partnership involved practicing scientists supporting high school students and their teachers in a curriculum unit focused on understanding the function of genes in plants. After an initial face to face introductory session the scientists supported classwork by providing wild-type and genetically modified plant seeds, information about how genes had been altered in the seeds, answering students' questions via email and the PREP program website, and providing short videos of their related research. They also revisited classrooms for a prolonged period towards the end of the 8-week long investigation, working 1-1 and in small groups with the students and helping with observations and collecting and analyzing data. Critical to the success of this partnership was the manner in which teachers and scientists worked together "promoting the idea of a scientific community" (Peker & Dolan, p. 235) through which meaning was negotiated via conceptual, pedagogical, social and epistemological acts. These acts created an effective structure for students to build conceptual understandings through learning designs, pedagogical strategies and social interactions that optimized the knowledge and capabilities of both teachers and scientists. In the classroom, this manifest in the generation of "common understandings of terms, concepts and practices, as well as by referring to others' results and using scientific terminology in ways that encouraged students' use of terminology" (Peker & Dolan, 2012, p. 235). The study identified the importance in successful partnerships of clearly articulated and understood roles and functions of scientists and teachers – or as Peker and Dolan describe "the division of labor" (p. 242), especially when the time scientists are able to spend in the classroom is limited. They comment that doing this at the outset can optimize potential partnership benefits, especially from shorter interactions.

The importance of establishing 'common ground' between scientists and teachers in partnerships is a recurring theme in literature (e.g., Brown et al., 2014; Nelson, 2005). Nelson's (2005) interesting study explored the impact dialogue had on the establishment and effectiveness of partnerships, particularly its influence on perceptions of power, status and control. The National Science Foundation funded project researched multiple case studies of partnerships in which graduate science and engineering students (STEM fellows) worked alongside grades 6-9 middle school teachers and students for at least 15 hours per week, in a 4-week unit of learning. The aims of the project were to enhance teachers' conceptual knowledge and support their transition to more inquiry-based pedagogies, and assist in developing the fellows' capabilities as science educators and their knowledge of the school system. Nelson analyzed the dialogic interactions of fellows and teachers across the cases, examining how knowledge building was facilitated or inhibited by dialogic interactions she identified as knowledge *negotiation, consultation* and *rejection.*

Negotiation described dialogic interaction where both scientists and teachers displayed deliberate intent to understand each other's knowledge and epistemic representations, contributing to the co-construction of learning content and pedagogical approaches of relevance and engaging for the students. Knowledge consultation was more unidirectional in nature, where one individual's knowledge was made available to the other, according to short term or immediate needs. This form of interaction was not co-constructive in nature, but was useful in progressing the planning and execution of partnerships when specialist knowledge was required, at specific points in time. Lastly, knowledge rejection was represented by dialogue reflecting dismissal of the other's knowledge as irrelevant, incorrect, or at odds with one's own views. Typically, this reflected in unilateral decision-making, with no attempt being made to negotiate

74   *Garry Falloon*

common understandings or interact in a way that would support or transform the other's knowledge development.

Nelson's (2005) findings indicated a prevalence of knowledge *consultation* in the partnerships, with limited evidence also being found of *rejection* and *negotiation.* She attributed some of this to historical relationships between teachers and university researchers that generally positioned teachers as the recipients and 'enactors' of researchers' knowledge, holding limited agency and influence over specific aspects of the partnerships. Nelson concluded that dialogic interactions in which knowledge was negotiated was fundamental to successful partnerships, as it facilitated the formation of a 'shared space' within which teachers and scientists could "encounter and confront assumptions together" (2005, p. 394), rather than problematize or dismiss the other's perspectives or contributions. She recommends consideration be given to specific activities including seminars, sharing of experiences, and opportunities to communicate perspectives on science learning, that could support greater understanding and assist in creating partnerships reflecting "more equitable opportunities for co-participatory professional development experiences" (2005, p. 394).

ASSESSING THE IMPACT OF SCHOOL-SCIENTIST PARTNERSHIPS (SSPs)

According to Painter et al. (2006), limited empirical evidence exists beyond anecdotal reports of the impact and outcomes from SSPs. However, significant research has been carried out investigating students' views of science and scientists, and many of these have employed instruments such as the Draw-a-Scientist-Test (DAST) (Chambers, 1983) or more recently, the Draw-a-Scientist-Test-Checklist (DAST-C) (Finson, Beaver & Cramond, 1995). In the original DAST, students were given a 'blank sheet' and asked to draw what they consider a scientist looks like, and in some variations - what a scientist looks like, *at work* (Huber &

The Problem of Perception

Burton, 1995). Student responses were then compared with listed stereotypical attributes, defined as:

> ... a lab coat (usually but not necessarily white), eyeglasses, facial hair (including beards, moustaches or abnormally long side-burns), symbols of research: scientific instruments and laboratory equipment of any kind, symbols of knowledge: principally books and filing cabinets, relevant captions: formulae, taxonomic classification, the "eureka" syndrome, etc. (Chambers, 1983, p. 258)

Chambers validated the DAST in a pioneering study that spanned 11 years and involved nearly 5,000 students in 186 classrooms from Canada, the United States and Australia. The study sought to determine at what age stereotyped images of scientists began to emerge, and any influences on the formation of these - such as gender, socio-economic status, intelligence and cultural background. Results highlighted the early emergence of stereotypical attributes, with some students as young as six identifying at least one of the seven attributes. This figure increased rapidly, so that by the time students were 10, scores had reached a mean of 3.26 attributes. The study also revealed the 'gender-typing' of scientists as Caucasian males. Despite half of respondents being female, only 28 women scientists were drawn – and all of these were drawn by girls.

In 1995, Finson et al. expanded the DAST to incorporate additional elements not included in the original test. These provided for alternative images, and took into account attributes including gender and race, indicators of danger, mythical stereotypes such as the 'Mad Scientist' or 'Frankenstein', indications of secrecy, and scientists working indoors or in underground laboratories. The modified instrument known as the DAST-C, was accompanied by a checklist, through which raters assigned points according to the presence or not of a particular attribute – the higher the score, the more stereotyped the image. In piloting the DAST-C with two groups of 12-13 year old students (one control group and one experiment group) Finson et al. (1995) determined it to be an effective instrument for identifying change in students' perceptions, following a structured intervention involving only the experiment group. The partnership comprised a series of teacher and student interactions with university and practicing scientists, involving "group and individual laboratory activities and detailed science discussions with science faculty; they also worked with faculty mentors on student-selected research projects" (Finson et al., 1995, p. 197). Following the pilot, Finson et al. argued DAST-C's reliability as an instrument for determining perception change, and at the same time highlighted the benefit of "involving students actively in science and providing them contact with practicing scientists on a regular basis" (1995, p. 201).

Despite the relatively widespread use of the DAST, Boylan, Hill and Wallace (1992) alert to issues about its accuracy "because it taps only part of the children's understanding" (p. 466). They point to limitations of using a drawing alone to make an assessment, and comment that the lack of context around the task, and the fact that respondents are required to *select* from attributes such as age, race, sex, dress, and setting "indicate that there is such a thing as a 'typical scientist', and that the subject is to represent such a solitary image" (Boylan et al., 1992, p. 466). They also claim that the test may only reveal respondents' knowledge of the *public* stereotype, rather than their *privately-held* views. Similar criticisms of the DAST-C have been levelled by Farland-Smith (2012) and Hillman et al. (2014), who comment on the inadequacy of drawings alone for accurately reflecting stereotypical thinking. Specifically, Hillman et al. (2014) voiced concerns about the influence of drawing skills on the students' capacity to represent "attitudes which are typically multidimensional" (2014, p. 2583), adding that this could result in drawings with little detail scoring lowly on the scale, but do not accurately reflect students' perceptions. Hillman et al. (2014) suggest that while the DAST is useful as a 'blunt instrument' for providing initial indications of stereotypical attributes, it is important that additional data are collected using other methods to verify its findings.

The next section describes and reports outcomes from a six-month school-scientist partnership involving a group of practicing scientists from SCION, a New Zealand government-funded Crown Research Institute

(CRI)[1], and 9 and 10 year old students from a regional New Zealand primary school. The partnership was funded by a government grant from New Zealand's Ministry of Science and Innovation (MSI) and was part of a 6 year initiative known as Science-for-Life, which was described as "an intervention program for schools and teachers to develop partnerships between schools and Crown Research Institutes (CRIs) to enhance science education and science literacy" (Dunningham, Falloon & Barnard, 2011). The study used a variation of the DAST-C supported by a short response questionnaire and semi-structured interviews to investigate any impact the partnership had on students' views of scientists and the nature of their work.

RESEARCH QUESTIONS

Data were collected responding to these questions:

1) To what extent did students hold stereotypical views of scientists and their work?
2) What impact, if any, did the partnership have on these views?
3) What key findings from the study are valuable for informing the establishment and execution of school-scientist partnerships?

RESEARCH CONTEXT AND BACKGROUND

The study involved five classes of year five and six students (9-10 year olds) and their teachers (Sue, Lisa, Charlotte, Sam and Ben - pseudonyms used throughout) from a regional primary school, located in a medium-sized city in the Bay of Plenty region of New Zealand. The partnership was negotiated after the principal approached SCION for assistance with developing the school's science curriculum, and indicated a willingness to enter into a longer-term relationship with the Institute funded by a grant

---

[1] For further information on the work of SCION, please see www.scionresearch.com.

78 *Garry Falloon*

from New Zealand's Ministry of Science and Innovation. The school was located within 5km of the Institute, which made logistical considerations manageable. The total number of participating students was 164, and they were involved in a school-wide science topic focused on *Sustainability*. The six-month topic explored social, economic and science-based (environmental) themes relating to sustainability, with the main partnership component focusing on *renewable energy sources*. SCION scientists were involved with the classes in a range of different interactions during the six-month period. These included facilitating field studies in a nearby Redwood forest, involving students in experiments about byproducts from the combustion of fossil fuels, setting up simple hydroponic gardens, explaining and describing their work in biofuel production, and teaching students about renewable and non-renewable energy sources. Students also got the opportunity to spend time in scientists' laboratories observing and asking questions about their work, and were given a tour of the SCION facilities.

The SCION partnership team comprised three female and one male scientist. They were Lucy (aged 25)– a GIS specialist with knowledge in biotic components of ecosystems; Maree (aged 29)– a soil scientist specializing in waste management; and Lisa (aged 32) – a molecular microbiologist. The male scientist, David (aged 37), was a GIS specialist and the team leader. The SCION team worked with the teachers and students for approximately four hours per week over the six-month period. The study conformed with SCION ethical guidelines for educational research, and in reporting and discussing data, identifying information has been removed to maintain confidentiality.

DATA METHODS AND COLLECTION

The research adopted a case study methodology using mixed methods for data collection and analysis. The DAST-C was administered to determine any changes in the number and type of stereotypical attributes present, pre to post partnership. This was supplemented by a short response

The Problem of Perception 79

questionnaire (pre and post partnership) and semi-structured interviews with selected students (post-partnership) to reveal further insights into their views of science and scientists, and to clarify attributes recorded in the drawings. The attributes selected were those included in Finson et al.'s (1995) original DAST-C checklist.

They were the presence of:

- Lab coat (white or other colour);
- Glasses or monocle;
- Facial hair (e.g., beard, moustache);
- Crazy hair or bald;
- Symbols of research (e.g., lab equipment);
- Symbols of knowledge (e.g., books, charts, files);
- Products of science (e.g., missiles, bombs, technology, inventions);
- Science captions and symbols (e.g., formulae, 'eureka', bulbs above head, lightning bolt etc.).

Obvious indication of stereotypical location was also noted (e.g., lab, cave, secluded or secret place), and whether the scientist was depicted as a mythical creature (e.g., Frankenstein, Dracula, werewolf, mutant). The teachers administered the DAST-C and short response questionnaire to students a week before the partnership began (see Appendix 1). This was supported by initial oral instructions for completing the drawing task. The procedure was repeated in the week following the final interaction - a school presentation to parents and the community of students' learning from the partnership. Due to absences on the days of administration, a total of 152 paired responses were obtained over four separate completion sessions. Of these, 80 were from boys, and 72 from girls.

DATA CODING

Pre-partnership DAST-C drawings were duplicated, and the researcher and a research assistant (RA) blind coded a random sample of 50 drawings using Finson et al.'s (1995) checklist. Consistent with Finson et al.'s guidelines, the presence of an attribute was only coded once – that is, multiple inclusions or examples within an attribute category were only coded as a single entry. Inter-rater agreement calculations (κ) were then performed on each attribute category, after which results were discussed and occurrences upon which no agreement could be reached, were discarded (Gwet, 2012). The full pre-partnership dataset was then coded by the RA, and results entered into an Excel sheet. Rater agreement results for the pre-partnership DAST-C drawings are summarized in Table 1. It must be noted that while the number of observed agreements is generally high across all attributes, this should not be confused with the number of attributes present in drawings. Agreement decisions included both the *presence* and *absence* of attributes, and in some categories, agreements reporting the absence of attributes substantially outnumbered those reporting their presence (e.g., symbols of knowledge).

Qualitative data from the questionnaires were coded by the RA using Braun and Clarke's (2005) inductive thematic analysis method. To facilitate this, the RA read all questionnaire responses, circling keywords and phrases describing, reporting or illustrative of scientists and/or the nature of their work. At this point, a randomly selected sample of 30 questionnaires containing the circled keywords and phrases was duplicated. These were used later for determining rater agreement. The keywords and phrases were then categorized to define first level themes. First level themes were identified relating to:

1) The physical characteristics of scientists (e.g., appearance, including dress);
2) The cognitive characteristics of scientists (e.g., intelligence, ways of thinking, qualifications);
3) The employment or activity characteristics of scientists (e.g., their work, where they work, how they work);
4) The personal characteristics of scientists (e.g., attitudes, dispositions, interpersonal skills, relationships, what 'type' of person they are);

The Problem of Perception

5) The contributions of scientists (e.g., what scientists have done for the world, what scientists have produced).

Table 1. Rater agreement for sample DAST-C data (pre-partnership)

Attribute	Observed agreements	SE kappa	CI @95%	kappa (κ)	Agreement strength (Landis & Koch, 1975)
Lab coat (white or other colour)	44	0.109	0.501-927	0.714	substantial
Glasses or monocle	40	0.090	0.692-1.000	0.869	almost perfect
Facial hair (e.g., beard, moustache)	42	0.118	0.401-863	0.632	substantial
Crazy hair or bald	33	0.114	0.500-0.946	0.723	substantial
Symbols of research (e.g., lab equipment)	46	0.104	0.576-0.985	0.781	substantial
Symbols of knowledge (e.g., books, charts, files)	41	0.129	0.310-0.816	0.563	moderate
Products of science (e.g., missiles, bombs, technology, inventions)	43	0.126	0.381-0.876	0.628	substantial
Science captions and symbols	43	0.118	0.430-0.891	0.660	substantial
Located in lab, cave etc.	38	0.123	0.263-0.744	0.503	moderate
Depicted as mythical creature	42	0.117	0.403-0.863	0.633	substantial

Samples of keywords and phrases aligned with the themes are recorded in Table 3, column 2. The RA then re-coded the questionnaires, this time tagging the circled keywords or phrases as negative (stereotyped), neutral (non-aligned descriptive), or positive (affirming, supportive, helpful). Multiple keywords or phrases in sentences or strings were coded as separate occurrences. Once this was completed the researcher accessed the earlier duplicated sample of questionnaires and reviewed the circled keywords and phrases, tagging each using the same code labels (negative, neutral, positive). RA/researcher agreement calculations were also performed on these decisions. Table 2 contains an aggregated summary of these results across the 5 themes.

Table 2. Rater agreement for sample questionnaire responses across the 5 themes

Response classification	Observed agreements	SE kappa	CI @95%	kappa (κ)	Agreement strength (Landis & Koch, 1975)
Negative (stereotyped)	75	0.086	0.466-0.802	0.634	substantial
Neutral (non-aligned descriptive)	43	0.118	0.430-0.891	0.660	substantial
Positive (affirming, supportive)	59	0.096	0.437-0.814	0.625	substantial

Table 3 presents illustrative coded data aligned with the 5 themes. The first and second columns (respectively) record the theme and sample keywords used to identify excerpts from responses, while columns 3-5 contain verbatim transcriptions from responses corresponding to each of the classifications. Some responses contained excerpts applicable to more than one theme and were therefore coded under multiple themes. For example excerpts from *"Scientists are cool people because they're really intelligent, and they get to make things that are helpful"* (student 147, item 4) were coded under 3 themes: personal characteristics (*cool people*), cognitive characteristics (*intelligent*) and contributions of scientists (*make things that are helpful*). Multiple excerpts were totaled in the analysis (see Table 5), however, for clarity, in Table 3 these have only been included under one theme. The above process was repeated for post-partnership data, allowing comparisons to be made between datasets. Interview data from selected students (n=16) were transcribed, but due to the relatively small number they were not coded thematically, but instead used to supplement and elaborate on data from the other two instruments. In reporting results, relevant verbatim excerpts from the interviews have been included to illustrate points made.

Table 3. Examples of questionnaire data coded in each category

Theme	Sample key words/phrases (from data)	Sample data coded as negative (stereotyped)	Sample data coded as neutral (non-aligned, descriptive)	Sample data coded as positive (affirming, supportive, helpful)
Physical characteristics	big head, bald, glasses, handsome, thin, pale, white coat(ed), unshaven, squinty, fuzzy hair, whiskers, wrinkled, old clothes, like you and me.	*"They are usually bald. It's because of the chemicals they work with all the time" (student 71, B, item 1).* *"Most scientists are men and they wear white coats and have sticking up hair... like in Back to the Future 2" (student 40, B, item 1).*	*"They kind of look like ordinary people, but not quite" (student 12, G, item 2).* *"They are usually old... but some can be young too" (student 31, G, item 2).* *"Some people think they look weird, but they don't have to" (student 69, B, item 2)*	*"Scientists look like you and me, except they do science things..."* *(student 8, G, item 2).* *"... and they don't have to wear white coats. They might wear them sometimes to protect their clothes though" (student 53, G, item 2).* *"They are normal people who do science stuff" (student 88, B, item 2).*
Cognitive characteristics	bright, brainy, crazy, intelligent, smart, worried, knows stuff, clever, dumb, mad, brilliant, insane, creative, intense, focused, dazed, forget things.	*"They're crazy men who hang out in workshops and stuff" (student 103, B, item 1).* *"When you see them on TV they look kind of intense and worried. They usually talk about disasters like earthquakes and things (student 92, B, item 2).* *"Scientists look funny. They always look puzzled" (student 86, G, item 1)*	*"They have to work hard to learn a lot of stuff" (student 122, B, item 2).* *"Grandad (ex-SCION) knows a lot of things and he helps me with my homework. But sometimes he gets a bit muddled up because he's always thinking about other things" (student 39, G, item 2)*	*"Intelligent people who go to university to learn lots and study science so they can help solve problems" (student 37, G, item 1).* *"Bright people who have good brains. They make technology to help us" (student 11, B, item 1).* *"They use their brain well. They can remember a lot of facts" (student 80, B, item 2).*

Table 3. (Continued)

Theme	Sample key words/phrases (from data)	Sample data coded as negative (stereotyped)	Sample data coded as neutral (non-aligned, descriptive)	Sample data coded as positive (affirming, supportive, helpful)
Employment or activity (work) characteristics or environment	laboratory (labs), work hard, chemicals, nuclear, well paid, by themselves, gadgets, danger(ous), test tubes, computers, valuable, workshops, experiments, study, investigate, separate, teams (groups), devices, flasks, technology, do science things, apart (from others), machines, polluted.	*"... spend a lot of time in a lab by themselves" (student 140, G, item 3).* *"They work with a lot of computers and technology and stuff... in labs..." (student 61, G, item 3).* *"They're crazy men who hang out in workshops and stuff" (student 103, B, item 1).*	*"It's just doing another sort of job to everyone else" (student 14, G, item 4).* *"They can do their work anywhere, it doesn't have to be in a lab... they have to go different places to collect information" (student 67, G, item 3).* *"Scientists look like you and me, except they do science things..." (student 8, B, item 2).*	*"Some work in labs but others work outside, testing streams and the air and stuff to make sure it's safe" (student 4, B, item 3).* *"Scientists have to work together to solve problems... they need to share their knowledge..." (student 92, G, item 4).* *"They share their research on the internet so it can help others" (student 11, G, item 4).*
Personal characteristics	geek(y), nerd(y), weird, friendly, boring, alone, snobby, lonely, brave, vague, shy, helpful, powerful, funny, trust(ed), confident, happy, normal, secret, work by themselves.	*"...kind of geeky. My uncle works for (an agri-research company) and he's a real geek..." (student 137, B, item 2).* *"I think they must be quite lonely because nobody would talk to them" (student 60, G, item 2).*	*"Sometimes it can be kind of secret (the work scientists do), but it's usually good" (student 98, G, item 4).* *"My Dad works at SCION and he's funny. He's just a normal person" (student 131, B, item 2).* *"Scientists would be quiet people because they need to think..." (student 3, G, item 2).*	*"It would be good to be a scientist because people would like you and come to you for advice" (student 106, G, item 4).* *"People would like you because you can be trusted" (student 10, B, item 2).*

Theme	Sample key words/phrases (from data)	Sample data coded as negative (stereotyped)	Sample data coded as neutral (non-aligned, descriptive)	Sample data coded as positive (affirming, supportive, helpful)
			"…like normal people but maybe a bit smarter. That would make them happy." (student 70, B, item 2).	*"Scientists are cool people because they're really intelligent, and they get to make things that are helpful" (student 147, B, item 4).*
		"Grandad (name) worked for SCION… he was a bit boring because all he talked about was science stuff" (student 39, G, item 2). *"They're probably nervous in case they make a mistake in an experiment or something" (student 49, B, item 2).*		
The contributions of scientists	create, improve (health), build (bombs), fix things, make discoveries (discover), destroy, explain things, cure (diseases), kill people, new plants, weapons, invent, make new stuff, how things work, help people, solve problems, mutants.	*"They make bombs to destroy things…" (student 93, B, item 4).* *"Muck around with things from bodies to make mutants…" (student 21, B, item 4).* *"Scientists made nuclear weapons that can destroy the world…" (student 120, B, item 5).*	*"Scientists have done good and bad things. Sometimes they do good like find cures for cancer and stuff, but sometimes they do bad like making weapons to kill lots of people" (student 73, B, item 5).* *"Most of the time scientists do things that help the world, but sometimes they don't" (student 49, G, item 5).* *"They're quite nice people, but sometimes their ideas aren't used for good things… it depends" (student 150, B, item 5)*	*"Scientists do important work to help the world" (student 119, G, item 5).* *"They make new discoveries that help us find out how the world works" (student 83, B, item 4).* *"Make facts. Scientists work things out and make facts we can use" (student 101, B, item 4).*

Notes: B= Boy; G= Girl.

86 *Garry Falloon*

RESULTS

Table 4 summarizes pre and post-partnership results from the DAST-C. Attribute categories and individual attributes are listed on the left, while raw score (n) and percentage (%) totals for boys and girls (respectively) pre and post partnership are provided across the table. Classifications of gender and race that were not clear from the drawings have been labeled 'Undetermined'. The category of 'Other' in race includes all races that were recognizable but not Caucasian (e.g., African/African American, Asian). In the table, figures have been rounded to the nearest whole number. Table 5 provides a numerical summary of pre and post partnership data from the questionnaire, coded under the first level themes described above.

APPEARANCE AND PHYSICAL CHARACTERISTICS

Pre-partnership DAST-C results in these categories indicated students held moderately stereotyped initial views of scientists. Boys in particular identified 'classical' attributes of a lab coat (55%), glasses or monocle (89%), crazy hair or bald (84%), and symbols of scientific research (62.5%) in their drawings. Other attributes such as facial hair (17.5%), symbols of knowledge (9%), products of science (21%), science captions (15%), location (21%), and depiction as a mythical creature (21%) while not so prominent, were still present in many boys' drawings. Girls' drawings by comparison included lab coats (33%), glasses or monocle (57%), crazy hair or bald (40%), and symbols of research (52%). The only other category of note was the presence of science captions (15%). Although the ratio of boys to girls in this study was reasonably similar, DAST-C totals suggest boys held more initial negative and stereotyped views of scientists than girls. While there was some movement for boys between the pre and post assessments, the classical media-portrayed attributes of scientists as odd looking, white coated, bespectacled males surrounded by bubbling beakers and dangerous equipment, remained

The Problem of Perception   87

largely in place. This conclusion is supported by analysis of questionnaire data for physical and cognitive attributes. While overall these data recorded fewer excerpts containing negative or stereotyped appearance attributes post-partnership, substantially more were still present in boys' responses across all themes, and the boy/girl ratio of negative or stereotyped attributes actually increased slightly (Table 5).

Interestingly, post partnership questionnaire analysis suggests that while there was a significant decrease overall in boys' negative or stereotyped perspectives (from 321 to 231), the number coded as positive did not increase proportionately (from 204 to 235). This appeared to reflect a 'neutralization' in boys' perspectives (from 117 to 173), rather than a major shift from negative to positive views. Girls' perspectives on the other hand, reflected a more noticeable shift towards positive views, post-partnership (from 236 to 326). Acknowledging that girls held more neutral or positive perspectives to begin with, the proportionately greater increase in girls' post-partnership excerpts coded as positive, indicated the partnership was more effective in influencing girls' views towards positive perceptions than boys. Girls also tended to add more explanatory detail to their DAST-C drawings, including textual information that in many instances elaborated on details contained in their images. Figure 1 illustrates this, with the student (Amy) adding the statement "a scientist is just a normal person with a good brain, and doesn't necessarily have to have huge glasses, a lab coat, or sticky up hair. He/she will just look like you or me," to explain changes made to her drawing.

While stereotyped attributes such as lab coats (36%), glasses (54%) and strange hairstyle or bald (41%) were still present in post partnership drawings, when interviewed about this, some students offered completely reasonable explanations as to why they included them in their images. For example, when interviewed, Rita commented that lab coats were important to protect scientists' clothing, as many worked in environments containing chemicals and other substances that could damage their regular clothes.

Garry Falloon

Table 4. Pre and post partnership presence of stereotypical attributes of scientists

Attribute category and attribute	Number and percentage of boys including attribute				Number and percentage of girls including attribute			
	Pre partnership		Post partnership		Pre partnership		Post partnership	
Appearance and Environment	Boys n (%)	Boys (%)	Boys n (%)	Boys (%)	Girls n (%)	Girls (%)	Girls n (%)	Girls (%)
Lab coat (white or other)	44 (29)	55	36 (24)	45	24 (16)	33	18 (12)	25
Glasses or monocle	71 (47)	89	49 (32)	61	41 (27)	57	33 (22)	46
Facial hair (e.g.: beard, moustache)	14 (09)	17.5	06 (04)	07	03 (02)	04	00 (00)	00
Crazy hair or bald	67 (44)	84	45 (29)	56	29 (19)	40	18 (12)	25
Symbols of research (e.g.: lab equipment)	50 (33)	62.5	38 (25)	47	38 (25)	52	17 (11)	24
Symbols of knowledge (e.g.: books, charts)	07 (05)	09	03 (02)	04	03 (02)	04	06 (04)	08
Products of science (e.g.: missiles, bombs, technology)	17 (11)	21	08 (05)	10	03 (02)	04	03 (02)	04
Presence of science captions and symbols (e.g.: formulae, 'eureka', bulbs above head etc)	12 (08)	15	17 (11)	21	11 (07)	15	06 (04)	08
Located in a lab or equivalent (e.g.: cave, underground)	17 (11)	21	08 (05)	10	06 (04)	08	03 (02)	04
Depicted as mythical creature (e.g.: Frankenstein, Dracula, Werewolf)	17 (11)	21	17 (11)	21	00 (00)	00	00 (00)	00
Gender								
Male	46 (30)	58	59 (39)	74	17 (11)	24	31 (20)	43
Female	03 (02)	04	08 (00)	10	30 (20)	42	38 (25)	53
Undetermined	31 (20)	38	13 (08)	16	25 (16)	35	03 (02)	04
Race								
Caucasian	72 (47)	90	70 (46)	87	59 (39)	82	56 (37)	78
Other	00 (00)	00	03 (02)	04	04 (03)	06	05 (03)	07
Undetermined	08 (05)	10	07 (05)	09	09 (06)	13	11 (07)	15

Notes: n(%) = number of students who included the attribute by gender relative to percentage of whole group. (%) = percentage including attribute by gender. Sample size=152 (80 boys and 72 girls).

The Problem of Perception

89

Another student (Anna) suggested lab coats served hygiene and safety purposes, possibly preventing the transmission of bacteria or diseases beyond the laboratory:

> ... I see you've got a lab coat on your scientists... can you tell me why you've drawn these in your pictures? (researcher)...
> ... 'cos they might get stuff on their clothes when they're working... you know... they wear normal clothes – like you and me, but some of the things they work with could get spilled or something and make a mess. The coat protects them (Rita).
> Anna, can you tell me a bit more about your picture.... for instance, what's the coat for? (researcher).
> ... well, sometimes scientists work with dangerous bugs and diseases and things like that... (Anna).
> How does the coat help them, then? (researcher).
> ... it might stop the diseases getting out, or something... they won't take it home... outside the lab... and it would be washed each night (Anna).

Rita's pre and post partnership drawings are shown in Figure 2. Of note is that she has included both male and female scientists in her post partnership drawings, whereas her pre partnership image is discernably male and exhibits identifiable stereotypical attributes (hair, glasses, coat and apparatus). Again, when asked about this, she indicated the influence the partnership had on her views, suggesting the presence of three female scientists in the SCION team played some part in changing her perceptions:

> ... and can you tell me why you've drawn a boy **and** a girl scientist in your second picture... your first one looks like a man... (researcher).
> ... yeah, it was a man... ya (sic) can tell by the hair (laughing). Lisa (SCION scientist) worked with our group, so I drew her! She was cool... and she knew so much stuff. She was nice (Rita).

Table 5. Excerpt totals, pre and post partnership

	Pre partnership (keyword/phrase)			Post partnership (keyword/phrase)		
	Negative (stereotype)	Neutral	Positive	Negative (stereotype)	Neutral	Positive
Physical characteristics	193	83	91	106	105	115
Cognitive characteristics	46	69	159	39	82	179
Employment or activity characteristics	67	30	58	57	51	83
Personal characteristics	142	41	53	113	60	97
Contributions of scientists	55	43	79	29	63	87
Boys/Girls	321/182	117/149	204/236	231/113	173/188	235/326
Total	503	266	440	344	361	561

Figure 1. Amy's post-partnership drawing and description.

EMPLOYMENT, PERSONAL CHARACTERISTICS AND ENVIRONMENT

Questionnaire data for the employment and personal characteristics themes displayed slightly stronger movement towards positive than neutral views, and interestingly, this movement was similar for both boys and girls. This also reflected in DAST-C drawings where there was a halving in the number of attributes indicating scientists working in laboratories or other secluded places, with almost the same percentage decrease for both boys and girls. Post partnership responses to the question *'where do scientists work?'* indicated a much broader awareness of science activities taking place in other than laboratory settings. These included working outside completing field work or in the community, in factories, or in hi-tech facilities such as NASA.

Figure 2. Rita' pre (left) and post (right) partnership DAST-C drawings.

Unsurprisingly, given the focus of the teaching unit and the SCION scientists' backgrounds, most responses linked scientists' work to natural world contexts such as forests, water quality or agricultural research.

Neutral and positive excerpts in responses coded under employment or work activities displayed reasonably significant increases pre to post partnership (from 30 to 51 and 58 to 83 respectively). Negative responses contained excerpts associating scientists' work exclusively with laboratories or similar venues, while neutral responses contained no such excerpts, but at the same time did not specify alternative work venues or activities. Responses containing excerpts coded as positive indicated alternative settings and/or provided some additional detail of the nature of scientists' work, suggesting a broader, more inclusive perspective. However, while neutral and positive perspectives increased, this did not appear to correspond with a fall in negative or stereotypical views, but rather with an overall increase in excerpts coded in this category. While negative perspectives did decrease, the fall was modest (from 67 to 57). Substantial decreases in related classifications in the DAST-C (traditional science research and knowledge symbols and products) support the conclusion that the partnership broadened students' perspectives of science activities existing beyond the laboratory. This was mirrored by a halving in the number of drawings clearly associating science activities with laboratories or similar facilities. Notwithstanding these decreases, the presence of stereotypical science captions and symbols in boys' drawings actually *increased* slightly, post partnership (from 12 to 17). Analysis suggested that while fewer boys produced drawings depicting science activities in laboratories, those who did included more stereotypical captions and symbols in their images, perhaps indicating some entrenchment of views.

Personal characteristics related to dispositions, attitudes and personality traits of scientists, including interpersonal skills and relationships. Across all themes, response excerpts coded as neutral and positive in this category displayed the greatest percentage increase pre to post partnership (46% and 83% respectively), and the second greatest percentage decrease in negative excerpts (20%). Interview data pointed to the SCION scientists as instrumental in facilitating this change, with several students commenting on their ability to explain science ideas in simple terms, and their excellent interpersonal skills:

The Problem of Perception   93

> Can you tell me a little about the scientist who worked with your group... how did you find that...? (researcher)
>
> We had Lucy... she was a lot younger than I thought she would be... and she's really pretty (laughing). (Samantha)
>
> Did she help you learn things while you were outside or in the classroom... doing your measurements and other things? (researcher)
>
> Yeah... she knew lots... but you could understand her... (Samantha)
>
> Understand her? (researcher)
>
> She told us science things... so we could understand them. She didn't use big words and things like that... we knew what she was talking about. (Samantha)

Similar comments were made by other students, many of whom highlighted the scientists' skills in making science knowledge accessible, and personality traits that identified them as 'cool' or desirable role models. Undoubtedly the female-dominated SCION team of relatively young scientists who were both knowledgeable and aware of the need to communicate their knowledge to the students in an age-appropriate manner, strongly influenced this result.

Many positive personal characteristics in both pre and post partnership responses were also associated with cognitive characteristics, by reference to the intelligence and trustworthiness of scientists as important and desirable traits. Responses to questionnaire items 2 and 4 indicated most students viewed scientists as knowledgeable, and that generally they used their knowledge for positive and helpful purposes. Post partnership interviews revealed that scientists were perceived as creative and inventive people responsible for many good things in the world, and for solving difficult problems. Interestingly, three students made comments indicating an understanding of differences between scientists and their work and applications of their work, suggesting that negative impacts of science were not necessarily attributable to scientists, but to how the knowledge they create is applied.

For example:

> ... scientists give us things we can use. They help us find out about the world... but some of the things they find out... maybe... aren't used properly. (James)

> What do you mean… 'aren't used properly'? (researcher)
> Well… like… some of their discoveries are used to make bombs and stuff… but I don't reckon that would have been what they wanted… really… (James)

These responses indicated a level of separation of scientists *as people* from the application of their discoveries or products of their science, implying that just because sometimes science knowledge might be used for negative purposes, this does not necessarily mean the scientists who created the knowledge were terrible people.

GENDER

Despite the predominance of females in the SCION team, the partnership appeared to solidify students' views of scientists as male, with the number of drawings coded as male increasing by 28% for the boys and 82% for the girls, pre/post partnership. This increase was associated with a corresponding decrease in the number of previously 'gender undetermined' drawings, rather than any substantial movement from female to male images. This result was surprising given the female-dominated make up of the SCION team, and seemed at odds with some students' earlier reported comments on personal characteristics and dispositions. Unfortunately, the questionnaire offered few additional insights into possible reasons for the consolidation around male images, as generally the students used pronouns (e.g., they, them) or nouns (e.g., scientist/s) to describe scientists in their responses. During interviews, students were asked about their depiction of their scientist as male, with responses indicating gender alignment associated with perceptions of *leadership*, rather than necessarily *being a scientist.*

For example:

> I see you've drawn a man as your scientist… in both drawings… can you tell me why you've drawn a man and not a woman? (researcher)

The Problem of Perception 95

'Cos (sic)... well, in the first one... I just sort'a (sic) thought scientists are more likely to be men... you don't really see many ladies... like on TV and stuff... (William)
What about in this one? (the post partnership drawing) (researcher)
He was in charge... that's David... he was the boss... (William)

Stacey, it looks like you've drawn a woman scientist here (pre) and a man here (post)... why the difference... why did you change your scientist from a woman to a man? (researcher)
Ummm... David seemed to be the one telling the others what to do. He was the chief... (Stacey)
And did that make you think he was the scientist? (researcher)
Well... I knew the Lucy and Lisa were called scientists... but they seemed more like assistants... David did all the talking... (Stacey).

This finding holds major implications for the delivery of partnerships, which will be discussed later.

RACE

There was little change in students' views of scientists as Caucasian, pre to post partnership. While girls drew more images clearly identifiable as non-Caucasian, the number was still small, and changed little as a result of the partnership (Table 4). Other races represented in girls' images (pre and post partnership) were African/African American (n=6) and Asian/Chinese (n=3), while in boys' post partnership drawings, all non-Caucasian scientists were African/African American. Interestingly, two girls who drew non-Caucasian images pre partnership changed their drawings post partnership to clearly identifiable Caucasian scientists. Interviews suggested a mix of partnership design, DAST-C test and peer factors played a role in facilitating this change, with the students commenting on convenience, the make up of the SCION team, and other students' images as influencing factors:

... and can you tell me why you changed the skin colour of your scientist in this drawing? (post partnership image) (researcher)

... oh, umm... when I looked at Simone's picture... she hadn't coloured hers in – and Nicole hadn't either... and it was easier. (Emily)

But are all scientists European? Do they all have white skin? (researcher)

No... but most are... our scientists were, anyway (the SCION team) ... and the paper was white... so it was just easier to leave it (Emily).

In addition to peer influences and scientist team composition, this finding suggests the representation of race in students' DAST-C drawings may have been influenced by the selection of media and other resources used to produce the images. While it is unknown to what extent Emily's reason for race representation applied to other students, it does highlight issues with using the DAST-C alone to accurately determine such views. While prompting students at the outset to consider alternative races may mitigate the 'convenience' factor and any influence of media and materials, it could also skew results by suggesting to students that non-Caucasian drawings were preferred. Therefore, caution is needed when making race interpretations from DAST-C drawings alone.

DISCUSSION

This section discusses results relating to the research questions concerning the existence of stereotypical views of scientists and their work, and the extent to which the partnership influenced these. Assessing the degree to which these students held greater or lesser stereotypical views relative to similarly aged students is challenging, given the paucity of studies indicating age-related attribute norms. However, data clearly identifies a significant presence of attributes indicated in the DAST-C in this group, and that these appeared more consolidated and difficult to dislodge in the boys. Specifically, students' representations of scientists as Caucasian males appeared particularly resistant to change – a finding consistent with other studies of a similar nature (e.g., Fung, 2002; Newton & Newton, 1998; Song & Kim, 1999; Özel, 2012). Interestingly, while some studies have shown a positive effect on gender representations of

The Problem of Perception

scientists resulting from partnerships and other interventions involving females (e.g., Miele, 2014; Painter et al., 2006), no clear evidence of this was found in this research. Despite the SCION team containing 3 female scientists, significant increases were noted in male post partnership DAST-C images, for both boys and girls. Interview data suggested roles played by members of the SCION team may have influenced the students' views, with some appearing to equate team *leadership* with being *the* scientist. Relevant to this result is that David held a senior position in SCION, with the other scientists reporting directly to him. Reflecting on this, it would be fair to say the hierarchical nature of their relationship *did* reflect in classroom activities and interactions, that could have been interpreted by the students as the female scientists being subordinates. For example, David completed all whole class teaching by himself, with the other team members assuming support roles and restricted to working with groups. Very few opportunities were provided for the others to display leadership, and this may have affected how they were perceived by the students.

While not impacting significantly on gender and race stereotypes, the partnership did appear to have some effect on other attributes, such as physical features, appearance and work location. Again, these results mirror those of other studies, that have shown benefits from partnerships expanding students' views of the nature of science, where science research occurs, and the relevance of science to everyday life (e.g., Hillman et al., 2014; Painter et al., 2006; Shin, et al., 2015). Although appearance attributes displayed significant decreases for both boys and girls, boys' science captions and symbols actually increased slightly, while the number of drawings depicting scientists as mythical creatures remained static. However, evaluating the former of these results highlighted the somewhat 'blunt instrument' nature of the symbols and captions DAST-C attribute for judging the presence of stereotypical perspectives. Although the number of boys' symbols and captions increased post partnership, closer examination of these suggested some were included to provide additional information relevant to illustrating the scientists' work, or where their activities took place – rather than deliberately intending to communicate a stereotype. Interviews supported this conclusion, with one student

98   *Garry Falloon*

commenting on how symbols in his drawing (a periodic table on the wall) were specifically included to indicate the scientists' work as a chemist (student 56, interview transcript, November 17, 2018). Similarly, as recorded previously, some students' inclusion of a lab coat reflected pragmatic concerns about hygiene and the protection of clothing, rather than intending to communicate a stereotype. A lack of contextual information about the basis of student decision making suggests results of the DAST-C should be interpreted with caution, and where possible, triangulated with other data.

The partnership clearly had a positive influence by broadening students' perspectives on the work of scientists existing beyond the laboratory. The number of drawings featuring laboratories or equivalent venues halved pre to post partnership, and perhaps more notably, several students included alternative venues such as forests, green spaces and industries (e.g., NASA) in post partnership drawings. This decrease is consistent with earlier studies reporting results from scientists working in classrooms (e.g., McCarthy, 2015; Miele, 2014), although these did not specify the replacement of locations with others reflecting a broader perspective. It is likely the decrease in stereotypical locations in this study was attributable to the nature of the teaching unit that involved the students and scientists in much outside and field data investigation and collection (Figures 3 and 4). Questionnaire responses provided evidence of this change, with excerpts illustrating how the partnership challenged students' views, normalizing their perceptions of scientists as regular people, 'who (just) do science things' and work in different places (Table A, row 3, columns 4-5). Again, this result illustrates the importance of using multiple measures to improve the accuracy of judgements.

Finally, Nelson (2012) comments effective partnerships rely on scientists and teachers negotiating a 'common space' within which collaborations can be planned and executed. This relies on parties understanding and appreciating the expertise and contribution the other can make to achieving partnership goals, and the extent to which roles are defined and agreed to. Sirotnik and Goodlad (1988) describe partnerships as symbiotic relationships, characterized by reciprocal benefits and mutual interdependence. In practice, Peker and Dolan (2012) argue this means that scientists and teachers need to "present themselves as knowledge authorities and promote the idea of scientific community" (p. 235) by agreeing to conceptual (knowledge), social (recognizing knowledge authority), pedagogical (ways of teaching) and epistemological (perspectives on knowledge construction) approaches to the partnership.

Figure 3. David and students setting up a transect for the bush investigation.

To achieve this, Peker and Dolan (2012) argue it is essential that scientists and teachers see themselves as equals in the relationship – each having their own particular expertise and skills to bring to the partnership and operationalize in delivering student outcomes.

Figure 4. Students using a flow meter tube to observe water quality.

In this partnership, the teachers clearly benefited from having scientists in the classroom in terms of expanding their own conceptual and content knowledge, and learning more about scientific procedures and methods. The scientists also supplied specialist resources such as transect grids, water quality monitoring and digital measurement and datalogging equipment, unavailable in the school. There were also observable benefits for students, who engaged in indepth investigations of significant duration that allowed them to collect and analyze data over time, often related to specific activities they initiated within the unit. However, considering Nelson's (2012) concept of effective partnerships functioning in a negotiated and collaborative 'common space', this example represented more a predefined delineation or division of labour, rather than a merging of the expertise and capabilities of teachers and scientists into a single, collaborative team. In practice, this manifest in the scientists (principally, the lead scientist) assuming responsibility for 'teaching the science', while the teachers looked after class and group organization, management and other logistics. In this instance the 'common space' was negotiated around the most appropriate knowledge and skills each partner could contribute towards achieving partnership goals, as defined by the learning objectives planned for the unit. The draft plan was initially developed by the teachers, however the scientists were invited to apply their expertise by inputting to the learning objectives and experiences during pre-partnership planning meetings. While this approach might not be viewed as mutually beneficial or representing an integrated, fully collaborative partnership model as described in literature, it did appear to be reasonably effective in delivering the unit's learning goals.

While ideally partnerships should aim for the utopian position of being fully collaborative and demonstrate shared leadership, mutually beneficial goals, and equal partner inputs, in reality this is very difficult to achieve, or as Waschak and Kingsley (2006) describe, "a romantic ideal" (p. 6). However, as reasonably demonstrated by this example, useful partnerships can be forged that do not necessarily represent a *merging* of knowledge and skills into shared leadership initiatives of mutual benefit, but instead reflect a structure based on *complementary* capabilities, where partners have defined roles but do not perceive their role to be of greater or lesser value than others. In conceptualizing partnerships therefore, it is important to understand that they can take many forms in different contexts, and that designs based on complementary but different capabilities may be of as much value as those reflecting more fully-integrated approaches.

CONCLUSION

In summarizing this chapter, it is useful to consider what has been learnt from this collaboration in terms of the design, implementation, performance and evaluation of school-scientist partnerships, particularly for influencing students' views of science and scientists. First, the study revealed shortcomings in the DAST-C when used as a sole measure of assessing the influence of partnerships on students' stereotypical views of scientists. Without the addition of a questionnaire and interviews, it was impossible to ascertain with any accuracy students' reasons for their inclusion of what could be interpreted as stereotypical attributes in their drawings. Examples were present in drawings of DAST-C stereotypical attributes such as symbols of science and lab coats, that interviews revealed were included for completely valid reasons, such as clothes protection and contextual or informational purposes. Also, comments from some students indicated the base colour of the paper (white) may have unintentionally communicated a racial stereotype. In the absence of prompting otherwise, it appears at least some students simply left the paper white for convenience reasons. Therefore, while the DAST-C provided useful initial indications of student perspectives, its results should be interpreted with caution, and further measures adopted to investigate whether what is recorded in drawings represents actual stereotypical views.

Second, while gender composition of scientist partnership teams is important for broadening students' perspectives on inclusive engagement in science and science careers, this study also highlights the significance of how roles in partnerships are perceived by students, and how this influences their views on who is the 'real' scientist. In this partnership David led all whole class teaching sessions, while the three female scientists assumed support roles and only took responsibility for groups of students for practical work and field investigations. Data indicated this division had significant impact, with post partnership drawings and questionnaire and interview responses confirming a consolidation of views of scientists as Caucasian males. When planning partnerships therefore, it is important not only to consider the gender make up of teams but also roles within a team, to ensure leadership is shared and visibly represented to the students.

Third, the focus and content of the Sustainability teaching unit involved a combination of in-class and field investigation, which appeared effective for expanding students' understandings of venues for science and how science is relevant to their everyday lives. The lengthy duration of the partnership also helped students better understand the process of scientific inquiry, by allowing sufficient time to set up and monitor the progress and results of practical work. Acknowledging that funding enabling the scientists to spend considerable time in the school was provided by a government department, the benefit of a partnership of this length was also apparent in the establishment of excellent relationships between the scientists, teachers and students. This undoubtedly enhanced the continuity

The Problem of Perception 103

and coherence of the partnership, through supporting its seamless integration into normal classroom programs. At a practical level there was no need for the scientists to 'reestablish' themselves at the beginning of each session – they simply picked up where they had previously left off. Although this model may not be viable in other situations due to funding limitations and possible impact on the scientists' own research work, it does signal the value of longer partnerships for developing a more meaningful and effective learning program.

Finally, while literature theorizes effective partnerships are mutually beneficial interactions resulting from a synthesizing of the talents of teachers and scientists, it should not be assumed that beneficial partnerships exist only in a singular form, or are established by following a prescribed process. A partnership is a relationship between scientists, teachers and students, and like all relationships, differ in form and nature – what works well for some, may not work so well for others. The concept of 'mutually beneficial' should also be interpreted broadly, especially given the unlikelihood of scientists' own research directly benefiting from their engagement in schools. However, science organizations are becoming increasingly aware of the need to engage more with the public to communicate accurate knowledge about their work - both as a 'public good' obligation, and sometimes to dispel myths and misconceptions about their research. In this example, SCION was aware of the need to address some public concern about their GM research, and saw activities such as working in schools an important part of their mitigation strategy. Like the partnerships themselves, benefits can take different forms. In closing, this chapter has outlined the influence a significant school-scientist partnership had on primary students' views of science and scientists. While results against this marker were mixed, there was little doubt about the value of the partnership for supporting teacher and student learning in a curriculum area that historically struggles to gain traction in primary schools. It is hoped this chapter may provide some guidance for others considering engaging in similar initiatives.

REFERENCES

Avraamidou, L. (2013). Superheroes and Supervillains: Restructuring the mad-scientist stereotype in school science. *Research in Science and Technological Education, 31*(1): 90-115.

Balcin, M. & Ergün, A. (2018). Secondary School Students' Perceptions and Attitudes about Scientists. *European Journal of Educational Studies, 4*(4): 66-92.

Boylan, C., Hill, D., Wallace, A., & Wheeler, A. (1992). Beyond Stereotypes. *Science Education, 76*(5), 465-476. doi: 10.1002/sce.37 30760502.

Braun, V., & Clarke, V. (2006). Using Thematic Analysis in Psychology. *Qualitative Research in Psychology, 3*(2): 77-101. doi:10.1191/147 8088706qp063oa.

Brown, J., Bokor, J., Crippen, K. & Koroly, M. (2014). Translating Current Science into Materials for High School via a Scientist-Teacher Partnership. *Journal of Science Teacher Education, 25*(3): 239-262.

Chambers, D. (1983). Stereotypic Images of the Scientist: The Draw-A-Scientist Test. *Science Education, 67*(2): 255-265. doi: 10.1002/sce.37 30670213.

Dunningham, A., Falloon, G. W. & Barnard, T. (2011). *Science-for-Life Programme Description Document: Fulfilling potential.* SCION Technical Report #47029.

Eugster, P. (2007). The Perceptions of Scientists. *The Science Creative Quarterly*. Retrieved from www.scq.ubc.ca/the-perception-of-scienti sts.

Falloon, G. W. (2013). Forging School-Scientist Partnerships: A case of easier said than done? *Journal of Science Education and Technology, 22*(1): 258-276.

Falloon, G. W. & Trewern, A. (2009). Developing School Scientist Partnerships: Lessons for scientists from Forests-of-Life. *Journal of Science Education and Technology, 18*(6): 11-24.

Farland-Smith, D. (2012). Development and Field Test of the Modified Draw a Scientist Test and the Draw a Scientist Rubric. *School Science and Mathematics, 112*(2): 109-116.

Finson, K. (2002). Drawing a Scientist: What we do and do not know after fifty years of drawings. *School Science and Mathematics, 102*(7): 335-345. doi: 10.1111/j.1949-8594.2002.tb18217.x.

Finson, K., Beaver, J., & Cramond, B. (1995). Development and Field Test of a Checklist for the Draw-A-Scientist Test. *School Science and Mathematics, 95*(4):195-205. doi:10.1111/j.1949-8594.1995.tb15762.x.

Fralick, B., Kearn, J., Thompson, S. & Lyons, J. (2009). How Middle Schoolers Draw Engineers and Scientists. *Journal of Science Education and Technology, 18*: 60-73.

Fung, Y. (2002). A Comparative Study of Primary and Secondary School Students' Images of Scientists. *Research in Science and Technological Education, 20*: 199-213.

Gwet, K. (2012). *Handbook of inter-rater reliability* (3rd ed.). Advanced Analytics: Gaithersburg.

Hillman, S., Bloodsworth, K., Tilburg, C., Zeeman, S. & List, H. (2014). K-12 Students' Perceptions of Scientists: Finding a valid measurement and exploring whether exposure to scientists makes an impact. *International Journal of Science Education, 36*(15): 2580-2595.

Huber, R., & Burton, G. (1995). What do Students Think Scientists Look Like? *School Science and Mathematics, 95*(7): 376-376. doi: 10.11 11/j.1949-8594.1995.tb15804.x.

Jones, G., Howe, A., & Rua, M. (2000). Gender Differences in Student's Experiences, Interests, and Attitudes Towards Science and Scientists. *Science Education, 84*(2): 180-192.

Kahle, J. (1989). *Images of Scientists - Gender Issues in Science Classrooms: What research says to the science and mathematics teacher.* (ERIC Document Reproduction Service No. ED370785). Retrieved from http://www.eric.ed.gov/ERICWebPortal/contentdelive ry/servlet/ERICServlet?accno=ED370785.

McCarthy, D. (2015). Teacher Candidates' Perceptions of Scientists: Images and attributes. *Educational Review, 67*(4): 389-413.

Mead, M., & Metráux, R. (1957). The Image of the Scientist Among High School Students: A pilot study. *Science, 126*(3270): 384-390. doi: 10.1126/science.126.3270.384.

Miele, E. (2014). Using the Draw a Scientist Test for Inquiry and Evaluation. *Journal of College Science Teaching, 43*(4): 36-40.

Milford, T. & Tippett, C. (2013). Preservice Teachers Images of Scientists: Do prior science experiences make a difference? *Journal of Science Teacher Education, 24*(4): 745-762.

Moseley, C., & Norris, D. (1999). Preservice Teachers' Views of Scientists. *Science and Children, 37*(6): 50-53.

Nelson, T. (2005). Knowledge Interactions in Teacher Scientist Partnerships: Negotiation, consultation and rejection. *Journal of Teacher Education, 56*(4): 382-395.

Newton, L. & Newton, D. (1998). Primary Children's Conceptions of Science and the Scientist: Is the impact of a national curriculum breaking down the stereotypes? *International Journal of Science Education, 20*: 1137-1149.

Özel, M. (2012). Children's Images of Scientists: Does grade level make a difference? *Educational Sciences: Theory and Practice.* Special Issue (Autumn): 3187-3198.

Painter, J., Jones, M., Tretter, T., & Kubasko, D. (2006). Pulling Back the Curtain: Uncovering and changing students' perceptions of scientists. *School Science and Mathematics, 106*(4): 181-190. doi: 10.1111/j.1949-8594.2006.tb18074.x.

Peker, D., & Dolan, E. (2012). Helping Students Make Meaning of Authentic Investigations: Findings from a student-teacher-scientist partnership. *Cultural Studies of Science Education, 7*: 223-244.

Reap, M., Cavallo, A., & McWhirter, L. (1994). Changing Perceptions of Scientists among Pre-service Elementary School Teachers. Paper presented at *The Annual Conference of the Association for the Education of Teachers in Science*, El Paso, TX.

Rosenthal, D. (1993). Images of Scientists: A comparison of biology and liberal arts studies majors. *School Science and Mathematics, 93*(4): 212-226. doi: 10.1111/j.1949-8594.1993.tb12227.x.

Shin, S., Parker, L., Adedokun, O., Mennonno, A., Wackerly, A., & SanMiguel, S. (2015). Changes in Elementary Student Perceptions of Science, Scientists and Science Careers after Participating in a Curricular Module on Health and Veterinary Science. *School Science and Mathematics, 115*(6): 271-280.

Sirotnik, K. & Goodlad, J. (1988). School-University Partnerships in Action: Concepts, cases and concerns. New York: Teachers College Press.

Song, J., & Kim, K. (1999). How Korean Students See Scientists: The images of the scientist. *International Journal of Science Education, 21*: 957-977.

Sumrall, W. (1995). Reasons for the Perceived Images of Scientists by Race and Gender of Students in Grades 1-7. *School Science and Mathematics, 95*(2): 83-90. doi: 10.1111/j.1949-8594.1995.tb15733.

Tan, A., Jocz, J. & Zhai, J. (2017). Spiderman and Science: How students' perceptions of scientists are shaped by popular media. *Public Understanding of Science, 26*(5): 520-530.

Tanner, K., Chatman, L. & Allen, D. (2003). Approaches to Biology Teaching and Learning: Science teaching and learning across the school-university divide. Cultivating conversations through scientist-teacher partnerships. *Cell Biology Education, 2*: 195-201.

Thomas, J., Pedersen, J., & Finson, K. (2001). Validating the Draw-A-Scientist-Teacher-Test Checklist (DASTT-C): Exploring mental models and teacher beliefs. *Journal of Science Teacher Education, 12*(3): 295-310.

Thomson, M., Zakaria, Z., & Radut-Taciu, R. (2019). Perceptions of Scientists and Stereotypes through the Eyes of Young School Children. *Education Research International*, ID6324704. Retrieved from doi:10.1155/2019/6324704.

Tuschi, J. (2008). Volunteer Scientist-in-the-Classroom Partnership in Metropolitan Schools. *Science Scope,* (December), 20-25.

Waschak, M., & Kingsley, G. (2006). *Education Partnerships: Developing conceptual clarity for improving education.* The National Science Federation Research, Evaluation and Technical Assistance (RETA) project (NSF report # 02-061).

APPENDIX 1: THE SHORT RESPONSE QUESTIONNAIRE

Who are scientists and what do they do?

Name:..

1. What is a scientist?

2. What sort of people are scientists?

3. Where do scientists work?

4. What are some of the things scientists do?

5. Can you think of anything scientists have done for us?

BIOGRAPHICAL SKETCH

Garry Falloon is Professor of STEM Education and Digital Learning at Macquarie University. Previously he was Professor of Digital Learning in the Faculty of Education at Waikato University in Hamilton, New Zealand. His background includes 22 years teaching and leadership of primary and secondary schools in New Zealand, Education Foundation Manager at Telecom New Zealand, working with Microsoft in the Partners in Learning and Digital Learning Object projects, and as project lead for the New Zealand Government's $10m Digital Opportunities Project. His research interests include mobile learning, digital learning in primary and middle schools, online and blended learning, curriculum design, pedagogy and assessment in digitally-supported innovative learning environments, learning in primary science and technology, and educational research methods. Presently he is CI for the ARC Discovery Project: Coding Animated Narratives as Contemporary Multimodal Authorship in Schools, and the NSW lead for the Commonwealth Government's Principals as STEM Leaders (PASL) project. He has served on numerous advisory and writing panels for eLearning policy and curriculum development, industry and sector advisory boards, and the N.Z Prime Minister's Panel of Experts for Digital Learning.

In: Science Teaching and Learning
Editor: Paul J. Hendricks

ISBN: 978-1-53617-406-9
© 2020 Nova Science Publishers, Inc.

Chapter 4

THE EFFECTS OF DISCOVERY LEARNING SUPPORTED WITH LEARNING BOXES ON STUDENTS' ACADEMIC ACHIEVEMENT, COMPETENCES FOR LEARNING SCIENCE AND SCIENCE ATTITUDE

Hülya Aslan Efe, Nazan Bakir[2] and Rifat Efe[3]*
[1]Department of Science Education, Dicle University,
Ziya Gökalp Education Faculty, Diyarbakır-Turkey
[2]Science Teacher, Fatih Secondary School, Diyarbakır, Turkey
[3]Department of Biology Education, Dicle University,
Ziya Gökalp Education Faculty, Diyarbakır, Turkey

ABSTRACT

Learning through discovery is seen as an effective tool to enable higher level learning by enabling students to move away from being audience and act more independently and actively within the classroom. The aim this study was to investigate the effects of learning boxes on the 5th grade students' academic achievement and retention in the science

---

* Corresponding Author's Email: hulyaefe@dicle.edu.tr.

classes. In order to realize this aim, a quantitative research method including an experimental design was used. Students in the experimental group were taught through learning boxes during "let's solve our body puzzle" unit of the 5th grade science classes, while students in the control group were taught the same unit through the teaching activities framed in the national curriculum. The participants involved 48 (Experiment: 24, Control: 24) students attending a state secondary school in Diyarbakır-Çınar district during the fall semester of 2016-2017 academic year. The study revealed that students taught through discovery learning supported with learning boxes scored significantly higher in academic achievement in comparison with the participants in the control group after the 10 weeks of the experimental learning process. The post-test results showed a statistically significant difference between the male and the female participant students in experimental group. Developing tools used in science teaching in the form of learning boxes and integrating them into constructivist approaches is among suggestions of the research.

Keywords: learning boxes, discovery learning strategy, science, achievement, learning competence, attitude

INTRODUCTION

Educating individuals with certain competences that can help them to adapt to the developing and changing world is one of the main aims of educational systems. The national curriculum prepared by the Ministry of National Education (MoNE) in Turkey aims to raise individuals who are capable of self-expression, questioning the rapid changing world, innovative, producing original ideas, researching, group-building and group work (MoNE, 2017). Within the framework of this vision, the constructivist approach dominates the philosophy of the curricula prepared by the Ministry of National Education. Because the constructivist approach involves a process in which each individual can change their existing understanding and develop new insights so that they can use their knowledge. In the constructivist approach students move from being passive recipients of knowledge to become agents who actively involves in the knowledge building process (Elliott et al., 2000) that leads to the solution of complex problems by students instead of the mere memorization of the content (Marshall & Horton, 2011). One of the increasing constructivist practices in the educational environments is learning through discovery. Learning through discovery is seen as an effective tool to enable higher level learning by enabling students to move away from being audience and act more independently and actively within the classroom as an actor (Bruner, 1991). Bruner (1991) who emphasizes that knowing is a process, not a product and the role of teachers is creating learning environments that will support individual and group learning. He pointed out that the teacher should be a guide in the discovery of ways of accessing knowledge rather than presenting the available knowledge. According to Bicknell & Hoffman (2000) learning through discovery involves three main features; (1) to explain, solve, integrate and generalize the problem, (2) to make activities based on student centred interests and (3) to help the student to integrate new knowledge into the existing knowledge base. Within these characteristics, the necessity for learning science through discovery is revealed. Because science is a field of research and thinking that requires discovery skills, based on scientific criteria, logical inferences and questioning thinking (Hofstein & Lunetta, 2004). These cannot be realized with the learning methods that keep students passive or semi-active in the learning environments in which students seem to increase their theoretical knowledge base while, they lack the scientific process skills that would lead to the development of necessary qualifications the required in the related field (Li, Moorman & Dyjur, 2010). Students learning through the discovery reach the explanations based on the evidence and they can construct new knowledge with the information they possess (Hermann & Miranda, 2010). The construction of new knowledge is not the end of its cycle through the discovery. The cycle shows continuity with the sharing of knowledge and its use in life (Marriott, 2014). Learning through this aspect is one of the appropriate methods that can be used to improve the competences of students to understand the events taking place in nature, to understand the relationships between events, to establish new relationships and to predict untested events. This is supported by the findings of different studies in the literature that learning through discovery improves academic achievement in comparison to strategies based on passive learning methods (Tal, Krajcik, & Blumenfeld, 2006), develops active thinking and decision-making skills (Minner, Levy & Century, 2010) as well as effectiveness in developing conceptual and operational skills (Novak & Canas, 2009; Fraenkel, Wallen & Hyun. 2012). Also, learning through discovery provides students with the ability to conduct scientific research and develop their logical thinking skills. Thus, students' application and problem-solving skills are also evolving. In this way, the student acquires a culture of thinking and working as a scientist (Lynch, 1986). In order to achieve the desired success in learning through the discovery, it is necessary to use instructional material (Krisnawati, 2015). Because through the use of tools in teaching, students work actively while doing activities, make a great number of examples that fit their individual qualities, experience individual and group learning, work on the problem, use their creativity skills and capture an opportunity to work based on the discovery (Cnets, 2006). In addition, the use of teaching materials in the classroom environment enriches educational experiences and provides depth to the subject. In particular, the use of teaching materials has an important place in the courses where intense concepts such as science are difficult to understand and abstract. Bringing the world of abstract science, which does not fit into the class, into the classroom environment can only be achieved by using teaching material. It gives students the opportunity to learn by living and even by making them. Another reason for the use of teaching materials in science teaching is that they provide a real-life environment by affecting the sense organs. The application of science courses with the help of instructional materials is important in terms of contributing to the education of students who use scientific process skills, make sense of science, seek answers that satisfy their curiosity, produce and conclude the problem. Learning boxes are one of the teaching materials that can be used for this purpose. Learning boxes are educational materials that educational professionals use to create written, visual and audio materials to support learning by doing and experiencing. They are boxes designed to provide students with learning opportunities to develop different perspectives. The written, visual and audio materials in the learning boxes contain both a general overview and in-depth knowledge. In the literature there are studies showing that learning through discovery increases science achievement (Taraban, Box, Mayers, Pollard & Bowen, 2007; Gijlers & Jong, 2005), science learning competences (Arinda, Anhar & Syamsurizal, 2018; Balım, 2009) and attitude towards science (Taraban, Box, Mayers, Pollard, and Bowen, 2007). Also, it is reported that the use of teaching materials in science education increases science achievement (Sönmez, Dilber, Alver, Aksakallı & Karaman; 2006), science learning competences (Thair & Treagust, 1997; Preece & Brotherton, 1997), and attitude towards science (Koç & Böyük, 2012). However, there was not any study in the reviewed literature that integrates teaching materials into learning box format and integrates them into learning through discovery. The fact that the constructivist practices remain at the level of programs in general (Castronova, 2002; Fazio, Melville & Bartley, 2010) and the lack of literature on teaching practices through teaching for science increases the importance of this research. In addition, the lack of sufficient number of studies to integrate instructional material using learning techniques into learning through the discovery reveals the necessity of this study. In this direction, the aim of the study is to reveal the effects of the teaching strategy supported by learning boxes on 5th grade students' science achievement, science learning competences and attitudes towards science. For this purpose, the following research questions were sought.

1. Are there any statistically significant differences between the control group students' pre and post-test comparisons for science achievement, competences for learning science and science attitudes?
2. Are there any statistically differences between the experimental group students' pre and post-test comparisons for science achievement, competences for learning science and science attitudes?
3. Are there any statistically significant differences between control and experimental group students' post-test comparisons for science

achievement, competences for learning science and science attitudes?

4. Are there any statistically significant gender differences between control group students' post-test comparison for science achievement, competences for learning science and science attitudes?

5. Are there any statistically significant gender differences between experimental group students' post-test comparison for science achievement, competences for learning science and science attitudes?

METHODOLOGY

The design of the study was pre-test post-tests control group design, which is experiment design. This design was selected because it controls many variables inflecting its external and internal validity. The experimental design compared a control group using conventional teaching method framed in the national curriculum with an experimental group using discovery learning supported with learning boxes.

Table 1. Symbolic representation of group models

Groups	Pre test	Application	Post test
Control Group	A1, A2, A3	The method offered by current science curriculum	A1, A2, A3
Experimental Group	A1, A2, A3	discovery learning supported with learning boxes	A1, A2, A3

A1 = "Science Achievement Test," A2 = "Competences Scale for Learning Science," A3 = "The Test of Science Related Attitudes."

Participants

48 (K: 24; D: 24) 5th grade students attending a state secondary school affiliated to Çınar District of Diyarbakır Province participated in the study

in the Fall semester of 2016-2017 Academic Year. In the assignment of the randomized teaching method for these two classes, the teaching method for the control group class was envisaged by the current program, and for the experimental group the learning strategy was implemented with teaching through discovery supported with learning boxes.

Data Collection Tools

Three data collection tools were used to collect data. In order to measure the level of accomplishment achieved by the students about the unit "Let's Solve the Puzzle of Our Body" the "Science Achievement Test" (SAT) was used; to measure students' attitudes towards science the "The Test of Science Related Attitudes "(TOSRA) was used, and in order to measure students' science learning competences the "Competence Scale for Learning Science" (CSLS) was used.

In the research, the SAT used to measure the success of the students was developed by the researchers. First of all, a resource research including teacher's manual, textbook, subject-based research books, question banks, internet resources have been taken into consideration regarding subject gains. SAT was prepared by taking into consideration the 13 competences in the 5th grade Science Course Teaching Curriculum published by MoNE (Ministry of Education) (2016). At least two science questions, the total of which were 34 questions, were designed to measure each competence to ensure the scope's validity and they were submitted to the opinions of 1 faculty member of Department of Biology Education, 2 faculty members of the Department of Science Education, and 5 science teachers. The developed SAT was applied to 6th grade students in 2016-2017 academic year fall semester. 9 questions with substance difficulty and low item discrimination were excluded from the test. The final test consisting of 25 questions was used as an achievement test. The reliability analysis of the SAT was calculated by the split half technique. The reliability coefficient for half of this test was found to be .68. The reliability coefficient for the whole test was calculated as .81 with the

Spearman-Brown formula. When the item difficulty analysis of the academic achievement test was considered, the average difficulty of the test was .58 and it was found to be highly discriminative when the item discrimination was observed.

"Competence Scale for Learning Science" (CSLS) was developed by Chang et al., (2011), and it was adapted to Turkish by Şenler (2014). The Cronbach Alpha reliability coefficient of this scale was found as .93 by Şenler (2014). Data were collected from 107 secondary school students in 2016-2017 academic years in the school where the study was conducted for reliability calculations. The Cronbach Alpha reliability of the competences scale for learning science was found to be .89.

"The Test of Science Related Attitudes" (TOSRA), which was used to determine students' scientific attitudes, was developed by B. J. Fraser (1978), simplified by Chaerul (2002) and adapted to Turkish by Curebal (2004). The Cronbach Alpha reliability coefficient of this scale was determined as .84 by Curebal (2004). Data were collected from 108 secondary school students in 2016-2017 academic years in the school where the study was conducted for reliability calculations. For this study, the Cronbach Alpha reliability coefficient was calculated as .85.

Learning Boxes' Preparation Process

Overall, classroom textbooks used in Turkey are prepared for the global realities to be used in all regions of the country. The content of the education gets distant from the reality and the interests of the students when it is focused on texts. Therefore, it is pointed out that the distance between the students' real lives and the textbooks is one of the most important factors related to the failure of public schools (Silva, 2000).

The main objective in the development of learning boxes is to link textual theoretical knowledge with the application of knowledge. The teaching materials which are brought together with the theoretical contents help students to comprehend the interest of the students in their knowledge (Cardoso, Cristiano & Arent, 2009). For this reason, learning boxes were developed to help the science teaching process and to embody the concepts of science.

When creating learning boxes, firstly, a separate learning box was created for each week considering united annual plan of science course published by researchers in the academic year. When learning boxes were prepared, the gains of the unit called "Let's Solve the Puzzle of Our Body" of the 2016-2017 academic year science course 5th grade science lesson teacher guide book, 5th grade science textbook of MoNE, science textbook source books and web to help learn science were browsed. The content of learning boxes appropriate for achievements was determined as a result of comments received from two faculty members working at the Department of Science Teaching and eight science teachers; and learning boxes were prepared by researchers.

Application Process

The application process of the research was conducted by the researchers. A 10-week lesson plan containing the "Let's Solve the Puzzle of Our Body" unit according to the MoNE Science Education Curriculum (2016), for the 5th grade students were prepared with learning outcomes consisting appropriate sub-topics in the frame of learning boxes and activities. A total of 40 hours of experimental study was carried out, science course being 4 hours per week. In the research, the present teaching method was determined to the control group by the present program, and the experimental group was realized by learning with learning boxes. In the control group, teaching was carried out according to the principles proposed in the textbook prepared according to the curriculum of the Ministry of National Education. There was no intervention. In the scope of the method prescribed by the current program applied to the control group, "Let's Solve the Puzzle of Our Body" unit was explained to the students with the help of the slide. Visuals on slides were discussed. In-class applications of the activities in the science textbook published by the Ministry of National Education were carried out.

Unit preparation and end evaluation questions included in the science textbook of MoNE were answered in the class by question and answer technique.

In the experimental group, the unit was taught with the learning strategy supported by the learning boxes and the unit "Let's Solve the Wisdom of our Body" unit. Before the research, to which the method would be applied, was given information about the in-class learning of the learning strategy with the help of learning boxes, and a sample hour was applied in the science course. In this study, the learning steps determined by Jacobsen, Eggen & Kauchak, (2002) were used. These steps are listed as follows;

1. The teacher presents the samples.
2. Student explains the examples.
3. The teacher presents supporting examples.
4. The student explains different examples from his / her previous knowledge and relates them to the first one.
5. The teacher gives examples and reveals examples that are not appropriate.
6. The student matches the samples and detects the difference.
7. The teacher asks the student to emphasize the nature and principles of the examples.
8. The student identifies and establishes the relationship.
9. The teacher asks the students to find new examples.

Within the scope of this study, the teacher firstly determined the outcomes to be achieved. Then, the teacher, in the direction of the goal of the discovery, created the path of the first steps of the approach presented the examples and students wanted to describe the examples. Then the teacher gave additional examples to compare with the previous examples and students wanted to reveal different situations. Here, it was tried to provide students to analyse the information and to examine the samples. At this stage, it was ensured that the learning box was divided into groups and the activities in the learning box were done together with the group members and the learning box was studied. Afterwards, the students were asked to give their own examples. The students were asked to make contrast samples and to give examples again. Finally, the evaluation process was carried out. The evaluation of the course was carried out at the end of each course in the form of evaluating the activities in the learning box.

Applications were recorded with photos and camera. While preparing for the new week, the experiences of the previous week were used.

Picture 1. Students working with learning boxes.

Picture 2. Students working with learning boxes.

Picture 3. Students working with learning boxes.

Picture 4. Students working with learning boxes.

Data Analysis

Quantitative data were obtained from the SAT, TOSRA and CSLS results. Levene test was used for determine the variances' homogeneity. As the study group consisted of less than 50 people, the Shapiro Wilk test was used to check whether the quantitative data obtained from the measurement results came from a normally distributed population (Büyüköztürk, 2011). According to the Shapiro Wilk test results for pre-test comparisons dependent t-test was used. For post SAT and CSLS comparisons was used the Mann-Whitney U test. For comparisons of post TOSRA independent t-test was used. The dependent t-test was used to determine the difference between pre-test and post-test in-group comparison. Statistical analysis was done by using Statistical Package for the Social Science.

Table 2. The comparison of 5th grade students' pre-tests results for academic achievement, competence for learning science and science attitude

Pretest	Groups	N	$\overline{X}$	SD	df	t	p
SAT	Control group	24	11.83	4.12	46	.00	1.000
	Experimental group	24	11.83	3.54	46		
CSLS	Control group	24	4.22	.42	46	3.77	.000
	Experimental group	24	3.69	.53	46		
TOSRA	Control group	24	3.82	.50	46	3.28	.002
	Experimental group	24	3.36	.47	46		

Table 3. The comparison of the control and the experimental groups' pre and post-tests results for academic achievement, competence for learning science and science attitude on gender

	Pre-test	Groups	N	$\overline{X}$	SD	df	t	p
Control Group	SAT	Female	13	12,2	4,08562	22	.505	.619
		Male	11	11,3	4,31909			
	CSLS	Female	13	4,3	,45220	22	1.18	.249
		Male	11	4,1	,37206			
	TOSRA	Female	13	3,8	,51978	22	.025	.980
		Male	11	3,8	,51978			
Experimental Group	SAT	Female	13	13,07	3,42689	22	1.98	.06
		Male	11	10,3	3,23335			
	CSLS	Female	13	3,8	,53616	22	1.08	.292
		Male	11	3,5	,52847			
	TOSRA	Female	13	3,3	,54245	22	-.071	.944
		Male	11	3,3	,40004			

In Table 2, pre-test comparisons of control and experimental group students are given. It is seen that the academic achievement levels of the control and experimental group students are equal before the experimental study ($t_{46} = .000$, $p > .05$). Before the experimental study, it was found that competence for learning science levels of the control group students were significantly higher than the experimental group students ($t_{46} = 3.774$, $p < .05$) and the Cohen's d effect value ($d = 1.112$) was found to be great. Similarly, control group students' pre-test science attitudes levels were significantly higher than the experimental group students' ($t_{46} = 3.283$, $p < .05$), and the significance of Cohen's d effect ($d = .96$) was higher (Christensen et al., 2015).

Table 3 demonstrates that there is no statistically a significant difference in gender between pre-test academic achievement ($t_{22} = .505$, $p > .05$), competence for learning science ($t_{22} = 1.18$, $p > .05$) and science attitudes ($t_{22} = .025$, $p > .05$) levels of control group students. Also, there is no statistically a significant difference in gender between pre-test academic achievement ($t_{22} = 1.98$ $p > .05$), competence for learning science ($t_{22} = 1.08$, $p > .05$) and science attitudes ($t_{22} = -.071$, $p > .05$) levels of experimental group students.

FINDINGS AND DISCUSSION

Based on the research data, firstly, the change between the pre-test and post-test scores of academic achievements, competence for learning science and science attitudes was examined.

Table 4 shows that there was a statistically significant difference between the scores of the students in the control group in favour of post-test according to the results of the academic achievement pre-test post-test comparison of the control group students ($t_{23} = -7.61$, $p < .05$), and Cohen's d effect value was found to be ill ($d = 1.07$) (Christensen et al., 2015). This situation shows that there will be an increase according to the readiness level of students in science achievement. Therefore, it can be said that all the methods contributed to the success of the students included in the teaching process. However, it is known that the level of this contribution is higher in the methods that make the student an active employee of the learning process (Treagust, Chittleborough & Mamiala, 2002). There was no statistically significant difference between the pre-test and post-test comparisons of science learning competences (t_{23} = 1.31, p > .05). Similarly, it was determined that there was no statistically significant difference between the pre-test and post-test comparisons of the students in the control group in terms of attitude towards science (t_{23} = .29, p > .05). It can be said that the teaching method that the current program applied in the control group has a negative effect on students' science learning competences and attitudes towards science. Before the study, it was observed that the control group students' higher competences for learning science and science attitude fell after the research. This situation is very worrying. Because the level of competence for learning science and attitudes towards science are known to affect science achievement (Lee, 2004). Aladağ (2007) and Akçay, Tüysüz & Feyzioğlu (2003) emphasize that the methods in which students are passive in the learning environment are inadequate to develop positive attitudes of students towards science. In the process of implementing the teaching method which is prescribed by the current program, it can be said that the students have a passive status, they do not have the opportunity to manage their own learning and they do not have time to explore the points they wondered.

Table 4. Comparison of control group pre and post-tests results for academic achievement, competence for learning science and science attitude

	Control group	N	$\overline{X}$	SD	df	t	p
SAT	Pre-test	24	11.83	4.12	23	-7.61	.000
	Post-test		17.04	5.44			
CSLS	Pre-test	24	4.22	.42	23	1.31	.201
	Post-test		4.13	.49			
TOSRA	Pre-test	24	3.82	.50	23	.29	.770
	Post-test		3.79	.58			

Table 5. Comparison of experimental group pre and post-tests results for academic achievement, competence for learning science and science attitude

	Experimental group	N	$\overline{\text{X}}$	SD	df	t	p
SAT	Pre-test	24	11.83	4.12	23	-14.66	.000
	Post-test		20.91	2.65			
CSLS	Pre-test	24	3.69	.53	23	-8.41	.000
	Post-test		4.45	.42			
TOSRA	Pre-test	24	3.36	.47	23	-8.90	.000
	Post-test		4.04	.28			

Table 5 shows that there was a statistically significant difference between the pre-test and post-test academic achievement of the experimental group students in favour of the post-test (t_{23} = -14.66, p < .05) and it was determined that Cohen's d effect value of this difference is big (d = 2.90). Many studies in the literature show that learning through discovery has a positive effect on success (Koç & Böyük, 2012; Bilgin & Karaduman, 2005; Saka, 2004; Treagust, Chittleborough & Mamiala, 2002). According to Akgün (2001), in science courses, through observation, analysis and synthesis if the students are enabled with scientific thinking, research, investigation and evaluation, it will play a key role in increasing students' science achievement. As a matter of fact, within the scope of this research learning through discovery supported with learning boxes which is applied to the students, opportunities for research, discovery, examination and evaluation of new products through the use of materials are provided to the students, whereby supporting students' science achievement levels. It is also indicated that the use of visual materials in science teaching can improve the mastery of learning (Hoirina & Dahlia, 2015; Safryadi, 2016). In the research of Mahlail, Susilowati & Anggraito (2018), they state that learning through the discovery, supported by visual materials, improves science achievement by involving students in the active learning process. With learning through the discovery supported by learning boxes, students can be said to have an increase in their level of comprehension as they are included in the process of creating the information themselves by teacher guidance.

When Table 5 is examined, it is found that there is a statistically significant difference between the pre-test and post-test comparison of the competence for learning science levels of the experimental group students who had learning through discovery supported by the learning boxes (t_{23} = -8.41, p < .05) and Cohen's d effect value of this difference (d = 1.57) was found to be large. By learning through discovery, students play an active, creative and innovative role in constructing science-related concepts, laws and principles in an autonomous way using science learning competences (Ilahi, 2012; Arindai Anhar & Syamsurizal, 2018). Learning through discovery enables students to learn by using their competences throughout the learning process. In this way, students can understand the concepts, principles and generalizations related to science more easily (Mukherjee, 2015). In this process, encouraging the teacher to have learning experiences by exploring the concepts and principles (Slavin, 1994) led to the development of success and learning skills in research. In this context, it is emphasized that learning through discovery is effective in developing students' science learning competences (Arindai Anhar & Syamsurizal, 2018). Again, the students have a significant impact on the development of competences for learning science by touching the visual materials with learning boxes, bringing the materials together and obtaining a new product, and discussing with the group friends. In this way, it is thought that the learning boxes and the learning of the students by learning from real life in cooperation (Işık, 2007) also increase the learning competences of science. In implementing the learning process in the experimental class, the teacher prepared the students to accept learning materials and to link them to the students' daily experiences or previous learning. Thus, it was tried to provide students to develop their discovery activities. The discovery activities started with asking questions that aroused students' curiosity. According to the research conducted by Tran, Nguyen, Bui & Phan (2014), the questions asked by the teachers in the learning process lead the students to search for answers by discovering new knowledge. It is thought that the learning boxes used for the students to reach the right answers play a key role in the development of the science learning competences.

In Table 5, there was a statistically significant difference between the pre-test and post-test comparisons of the attitude levels of the experimental group students who were taught by learning through discovery supported by learning boxes in favour of the post-test (t_{23} = -8.90, p <.05) and Cohen's d effect value of this difference (d = 1.73) seems to be large (Christensen et al., 2015). This result shows that the learning boxes realized with the help of the learning through discovery by the 5th grade students are sufficient for the positive change in attitudes towards science. Similarly, Koç and Böyük (2012) found that students' attitudes towards science increased significantly after the study as a result of the studies they conducted with the 7th grade students in the primary school. In this situation, it can be concluded that the attitudes towards the science at the secondary school level may be increased in the teaching methods where the student is active by discovering, touching, and making. In addition, it can be concluded that because the attitudes develop over time in humans, it takes less time to change the attitudes of younger students. Since it will affect students' learning, encouraging them to have a positive attitude towards science is one of the important objectives of science teaching (Lee, 2004). This justifies the students' efforts to develop and improve their attitudes towards science in science teaching (Zint, 2002).

Table 6. Comparison of control and experimental groups post-tests results for academic achievement and competence for learning science

Post tests	Groups	N	Mean Rank	Sum of Ranks	U	p
SAT	Control group	24	19.56	469.5	169.5	.014
	Experimental groups	24	29.44	706.5		
CSLS	Control group	24	19.35	465.5	164.5	.011
	Experimental groups	24	29.65	711.5		

While the academic achievement levels of the control and experimental group students were the same before the study (Table 2), there was a statistically significant difference between the experimental and control group students' academic achievement test comparisons in favour of the experimental group (Table 6) (U = 169.50, p < .05). Learning by means of discovery; While providing students with the opportunity to become active participants in the learning process, it provides the opportunity to associate science subjects with real life, which provides students with a meaningful understanding of their academic achievements (Tretter & Jones, 2003; Inoue & Buczynski, 2010; Luera, Killu & O'Hagen, 2003; Ezejitu, 2009; Otobo, 2012; Teker et al., 2017; Njoku, 2004; Udo & Udo, 2007; Folounrunso & Sunday, 2017; Martins & Oyebanji, 2000; Bajah & Asim, 2002). Sembiring & Sihombing (2014) draws attention that discovery activities have a positive impact on students' learning. Minner, Levy, and Century (2010) synthesized 138 studies investigating the effect of learning on science achievement at the K-12 level published between 1984 and 2002. Fifty-one percent of these studies indicate that learning through discovery has a positive effect on students' structuring of science knowledge and learning of science concepts. Similarly, Bamiro (2015) emphasizes that learning through the discovery increases the students' success. In the study by Liu, Lee & Linn (2010), they concluded that discovery-supported science learning is more effective in improving students' integration of knowledge. One of the important features of learning by discovery is to ask students to explore the next step by asking questions. Seeking answers to questions means keeping students cognitively alert. In fact, Marriott (2014) emphasizes that students are more influenced by the teachers who keep the students active by asking questions. It is known that using teaching materials for science teaching in the classroom environment is one of the important factors affecting success. It is stated that the use of materials in science education is very effective in increasing the academic achievement of students (Ünal & Çelikkaya, 2009). Supporting science teaching with concrete materials, enabling students to work, and addressing different senses to students, supports students' academic achievement levels (Teker et al., 2017).

According to Saka (2004), the use of concretization tools is effective when support is needed in order to mobilize students' prior knowledge and to make meaningful learning. Arıkan (2009) in his study showed that the lessons learned based on visual tools increase student achievement and improve classroom environments positively. At the same time, Majid (2008) stated that the students were able to learn and manage systematically with readiness levels using appropriate learning material. Thus, the structuring of knowledge in the mind is supported. In this respect, it can be said that the learning boxes and the learning of science support the process of building new knowledge with the students' own pre-knowledge. As a matter of fact, students realize their own experiences to realize the activities of the discovery in the learning material (Hake, 2002). Thus, the learner organizes new information and integrates them with previously stored information. Students act as researchers in the learning environment supported by learning boxes; in doing so, the students place a newly introduced object in a previously discovered or defined category (Gallenstein, 2004). The majority of the activities in the learning boxes prepared for this research consist of colored visual materials. The reason for this was the development of activities addressing more sensory organs in order to make science students understand the 5th grade, who are in the age group of 9-10. Because Wulanzani and colleagues (2016) indicate that visual learning materials contribute 94.7% of students' learning. In addition, Safitri et al., (2014) stated that the learning materials that have visual elements support the learning efficiency. In addition, it is known that the effects of visual materials on the analysis and processing of existing information are available. Nasution (2009) emphasizes that learning supported by teaching materials is three or four times faster than oral learning. Ristiono, Novriyanti & Yudha, (2012) points out that visual learning materials increase the average 5% learning level to the level of 74%.

While the pre-test competence for learning science levels of the pre-study control group and the experimental group students were significantly higher in favour of the control group (Table 2), at the end of 10 weeks of instruction, it was found that the science learning competences levels of the experimental group students, which were based on learning through discovery supported by learning boxes, were significantly higher than those of the control group (Table 6) (U = 164.5, p < .05). Students with the ability to learn science can find solutions by asking questions about real problems (Bereiter & Scardamalia, 1989), can design and conduct a scientific research (Schauble, Glaser, Duschl, Schulze & John, 1995), can collect data and analyze (Hancock, Kaput & Goldsmiht, 1992; Vellom & Anderson, 1999), interpret the data and draw conclusions (Chinn & Brewer, 1993) and report the results (Singer, Marx, Krajcik & Clay Chambers, 2000). In this respect, science learning skills appear as an important part of science competences. Learning by means of discovery helps students to acquire advanced cognitive skills while creating and testing hypotheses on a sample they encounter in everyday life (Matthews, 2002; Abdi, 2014). It is thought crucial that experimental group students be allowed to be released under the guidance of learning boxes while they are learning science and manage their own learning. In addition, the fact that learning through the discovery supported by learning boxes keeps the student active with discovery activities from the beginning of the course led to the emergence of this result. In fact, Eriza, Ananda, & Ahda (2015) emphasizes that learning through the discovery develops students' learning skills. However, in the control group, in which the teaching method prescribed by the current program is applied, it is assumed that the activities where students cannot make their own decisions and draw their own learning pathways are insufficient in developing the competences for learning science levels.

Table 7. Comparison of control and experimental groups post-tests results for science attitude

Post test	Groups	N	$\overline{\text{X}}$	SD	df	t	p
TOSRA	Control group	24	3.79	.58	46	-1.849	.071
	Experimental group	24	4.04	.28			

When the post-test comparison of the attitudes towards science in Table 7 is examined, it is determined that there was no statistically significant difference between the attitude average of the students in the experimental and control groups (t_{46} = -2.44, p <.05). Control group students' attitude average of before the study (Table 2), ($\overline{X}$ = 3.82) was found to decrease after the study ($\overline{X}$ = 3.79). However, it was found that the attitude levels of the experimental group students towards pre-research science ($\overline{X}$ = 3.36) increased after the study ($\overline{X}$ = 4.04). This result shows that at the end of the science teaching carried out for 10 weeks, the experimental group students' attitudes towards the course increased by learning through discovery supported by learning boxes, but current teaching method applied in the control group negatively affect students' attitudes towards science. Since it will affect students' learning, encouraging them to have a positive attitude towards science is one of the important objectives of science teaching (Lee, 2004). Attitudes towards science lead to positive or negative feelings about science. There is a positive trend towards science because of the attitudes, learning and ability to be taught in science education (Zint, 2002). It can be argued that science teaching lesson materials, which generally contain abstract concepts, necessitate a teaching full of manual activities. Developing skills, learning activities filled with manual activities involve appropriate environments (Yiğit & Akdeniz, 2003). The most important feature of learning through discovery based on learning boxes is that it transmits the science environment outside the classroom into the box and creates appropriate, clear, concrete environments for students. In this respect, it is not surprising that the attitudes of experimental group students towards science have increased positively. By developing a positive attitude towards science with the students, they can be directed to this field (Castronova, 2002) as well as to the professions related to science (George, 2006). Again, the studies of Parker & Gerber (2000) and Mattern & Schau (2002) in this field show that the positive attitudes of the students have an impact on the study and research in the field of science in the future. It was also revealed that attitude and success were positively correlated with the attitudes of students towards science lesson (Parker & Gerber, 2000).

Widiadnyana, Sadia & Suastra (2014) found that learning through discovery was more effective in learning seventh grade students' science concepts. In the same study, it is pointed out that the attitudes of the students in the classroom with the learning by discovery increased significantly. In addition, Safitri et al., (2014) stated that learning materials which have visual elements support students' positive attitude towards science lesson.

When we look at Table 8, it is seen that there is no statistically significant difference between the post-test academic achievement of the control group students according to gender variable (t_{22} = 1.09, p > .05). Similarly, it was found that there was no statistically significant difference between the mean scores of the post-test competences for learning science of the control group according to the gender variable (t_{22} = 1.74, p > .05). Again, it was found that there was no statistically significant difference between the control group students' mean scores towards the post-test according to the gender variable (t_{22} = .959, p> .05). It was determined that the current teaching method applied to the control group students increased the success of the girl ($\overline{X}_{pre}$ = 12.23; $\overline{X}_{post}$ = 18.15) and boys ($\overline{X}_{pre}$ = 11.36; $\overline{X}_{post}$ = 15.72), but there was no significant difference between these achievements. When the control group students' science learning competences' mean is taken into consideration, it is seen that the girls ($\overline{X}_{pre}$ = 4.31; $\overline{X}_{post}$ = 4.28) and male ($\overline{X}_{pre}$ = 4.11; $\overline{X}_{post}$ = 3.94) students have decreased their science learning competences' average after 10 week period. Also, on the basis of the averages, it was determined that the female students in the control group ($\overline{X}_{pre}$ = 3.83; $\overline{X}_{post}$ = 3.90) increased their attitudes towards science, whereas the male students ($\overline{X}_{pre}$ = 3.82; $\overline{X}_{post}$ = 3.67) decreased their attitudes towards science. These results show that the method that the current program predicts is insufficient to develop positive results in terms of gender.

Table 8. The Comparison of control group post-tests results for academic achievement, competence for learning science and science attitude on gender

	Gender	N	$\overline{X}$	SD	df	t	p
SAT	Female	13	18.15	5.41	22	1,09	,287
	Male	11	15.72	5.44			
CSLS	Female	13	4.28	.42	22	1,74	,094
	Male	11	3.94	.52			
TOSRA	Female	13	3.90	.59	22	,959	,348
	Male	11	3.67	.57			

Table 9. The Comparison of experimental group post-tests results for academic achievement, competence for learning science and science attitude on gender

	Gender	N	$\overline{X}$	SD	df	t	p
SAT	Female	13	22,1	2,46514	22	2,6	.01
	Male	11	19,5	2,25227			
CSLS	Female	13	4,55	,40970	22	1.22	.234
	Male	11	4,34	,42888			
TOSRA	Female	13	4,16	,31369	22	2.4	.02
	Male	11	3,9	,18187			

When Table 9 is examined, it is seen that there is a statistically significant difference between the results of the last test and academic achievement of the experimental group students and this difference is in favour of female students ($t_{22} = 2.6$, $p < .05$). This result shows that learning through discovery supported by learning boxes is more effective in increasing female students' science achievement. Şengül (2006) also emphasizes that gender is an effective variable in student achievement. In this context, in the literature, there are studies showing that male students are more successful in the group (Ekeh, 2004), or female students are more successful in the group (Galadima, 2003), and female and male students' achievements are equal when appropriate conditions are provided for learning (Udo, 2010; Udo & Udo, 2007; Omiko, 2016). Around the world, female students are getting closer to male students in science. Turkey also shows this trend. According to PISA 2015 results in Turkey, in general, female students show 6 points higher performance in science than male students, but this difference was not statistically significant (Batry in 2017).

It has been identified that there was no statistically significant difference between the post-test science learning competences' levels of the experimental group students according to the gender variable ($t_{22} = 1.22$, $p > .05$). However, it is seen that both the female students ($\overline{X}_{pre} = 3.80$; $\overline{X}_{post} = 4.55$) and the male students ($\overline{X}_{pre} = 3.57$; $\overline{X}_{post} = 4.34$) in the experimental group increased their science learning competences' levels on the basis of averages. It was concluded that according to the variable of gender there was a statistically significant difference between the attitude average of the experimental group students and this difference was in favour of female students ($t_{22} = 2.4$, $p < .05$). Based upon some of the results of empirical studies in which students are an active part of the learning process rather than being passive, some indicated difference towards the male students (Sungur & Tekkaya, 2003), some of them towards female ones (Galadima, 2003), while some of them indicated no gender-based differences between attitudes towards science (Koç & Büyük, 2012). It is thought that the difference in the literature may have been affected by the researched science units, age groups and socio-economic levels. In this study, the fact that female students have higher averages in terms of attitude towards science can be explained with learning by means of learning through discovery with learning boxes. Especially, the fact that this study rests on the unit called "Let's Solve the Puzzle of Our Body," which is a biology subject can explain that the female students are more enthusiastic. Özay, Ocak and Ocak (2003) stated that male students generally like physics, and female ones like biology lessons more. Pehlivan and Köseoğlu (2010), in their study on attitudes towards biology course, state that female students' attitudes towards biology course are more positive than male students and female students perceive themselves more successfully in biology course and they pay more attention to this course. In the study, it is emphasized that the biology course is liked more by female students and this may be because of the fact that the female students perceived themselves as more competent in the field of biology (Pehlivan & Köseoğlu, 2010).

CONCLUSION

The present study has documented that the contribution of the teaching methods prescribed in the current national curriculum, which does not include students' learning through discovery, has little contribution to student academic achievement in science classes. Also, this study revealed that the teaching methods prescribed in current national curriculum has a negative effect on students' attitude towards science learning skills and attitudes towards science. In contrast, discovery learning supported by learning boxes had a positive effect on students' science academic achievement. Likewise, the experimental group students,' who had the opportunity to work with learning boxes, science learning skill levels increased. Also, discovery learning supported with learning boxes was effective in developing positive attitudes towards science. It has been concluded that discovery learning supported with the learning boxes was is an effective method to increase female students' science achievement and attitudes towards science. Based the findings of the study it is fair to suggest that science teachers should be encouraged to incorporate learning boxes into their classroom practises to enrich their learning environments.

REFERENCES

Abdi, A. 2014. The Effect of Inquiry-based Learning Method on Students' Academic Achievement in Science Course. *Universal Journal of Educational Research*, 2(1), 37-41.

Akçay, H., Tüysüz, C. & Feyzioğlu, B. 2003. An Example of The Effect of Computer-Aided Science Teaching on Student Achievement and

Attitude: The Concept of Moles and Avogadro Number. *The Turkish Online Journal of Educational Technology. V: 2*, I: 2, A:9.

Akgün, S. 2001. *Science Teaching.* Ankara: Pegem A Publishing.

Aladağ, E. 2007. The Effect of Using GIS on 7th Grade Student's Attitude against Social Studies Lessons. *Journal of Turkish Social Researchs.* v. 11, n: 2.

Arinda, N., Anhar, A. & Syamsurizal, 2018. The Effects of Discovery Learning Model Nuanced Science Literacy Towards Students' Competence in Learning Natural Science, *International Journal of Progressive Sciences and Technologies*, Vol. 8, No. 1, pp. 96-105.

Arıkan, A. 2009. Visual Materials in the Teaching of Literature: A Short Story Application. *Journal of Ondokuz Mayıs University Education Faculty*, 27, 1-16.

Bajah, S. T. & Asim, A. E 2002. Construction and Science Learning Experimental evidence in a Nigerian Setting. *World Council for Curriculum and Instruction (WCCI) Nigeria.* 3 (1), 105-114.

Balım, A. G. 2009. The Effects of Discovery Learning on Students' Success and Inquiry Learning Skills. *Eurasian Journal of Educational Research*, 35, 1-20.

Bamiro, A. O. 2015. Effects of guided discovery and think-pair-share strategies on secondary school students' achievement in chemistry. *Sage open,* Volume 1.

Batrya, A. 2017. *PISA 2015;* Success through Gender Based in Turkey, Education Reform Initiative. İstanbul: Sabancı University, Centre of Politics. Retrieved from http://www.egitimreformugirisimi.org/yayin/ turkiyede-cinsiyete-dayali-basari-farki-pisa-arastirmasi-bulgulari/.

Bereiter, C. & Scardamalıa, M. 1993. *Surpassing ourselves: An ınquiry into the nature and ımplications of expertise.* Open Court, Chicago.

Bicknell-Holmes, T. & Hoffman, P. S. 2000. Elicit, engage, experience, explore: Discovery learning in library instruction. *Reference Services Review.* 28(4), 313-322.

Bilgin, I. & Karaduman, A. 2005. Investigating the Effects of Cooperative Learning on 8 Grade Students' Attitudes toward Science. *Elementary Education Online, 4(2),* 32-45.

Bruner, J. S. 1991. *Towards a Teaching Theory.* (Translated by: F. Varış ve T. Gürkan). Ankara: Ankara University Publishing.

Cardoso, D. C., Cristiano, M. P. & Arent, C. O. 2009. Development of New Didactic Materials for Teaching Science and Biology: The Importance of the New Education Practices. *On Line Journal of Biological Sciences*, 9 (1): 1-5.

Castronova, J. A. 2002. Discovery learning for the 21st century: What is it and how does it compare to traditional learning in effectiveness in the 21st century. *Action Research Exchange, 1(1),* 1–12.

Chaerul, A., 2002. *A study of student attitudes toward physics and classroom environment based on gender and grade level among senior secondary education students in Indonesia.* Doctorial Dessertation: New Mexico State University,

Chang, H. P., Chen, C. C., Guo, G. J., Cheng, Y. J., Lin, C. Y. & Jen, T. H. 2011. The development of a competence scale for learning science: ınquiry and communication. *International Journal of Science and Mathematics Education, 9(5),* 1213–1233.

Chinn, C. A., & Brewer, W. F. 1993. The Role of Anomalous Data in Knowledge Acquisition: A Theoretical Framework and Implications for Science Instruction. *Review of Educational Research*, 63, 1–49.

Christensen, L. B., Johnson, R. B. & Turner, L. A. 2015. *Research Methods Design and Analysis.* Aypay, A. (Çeviri Ed.). (2. Baskı), Ankara: Anı Yayıncılık.

Cnets, 2006. *Technology Foundation Standards for Students.* 10/07/2008. Retrived from http://cnets.iste.org/students/s_stands.html.

Cürebal, F. 2004. *Gifted Students Attitudes Towards Science and Classroom Environment Based on Gender and Grade Level.* Unpublished Master Thesis. Middle East University Institute of Science, Ankara.

Ekeh, P. U. 2004. Gender bias and achievement in Science and Mathematics among Primary School Pupils: Implications for human resource development. *J. Curr. Organ. Niger.* 11(2):30-33.

Elliott, S. N., Kratochwill, T. R., Littlefield Cook, J. & Travers, J. (2000). *Educational psychology: Effective teaching, effective learning (3rd ed.)*. Boston, MA: McGraw-Hill College.

Eriza, S., Ananda, A. & Ahda, Y. 2015. Pengaruh Model Discovery Learning Berbantuan Lembar Kerja Siswa (LKS) Terhadap Pencapaian Kompetensi Belajar Biologi Siswa Kelas VIII di SMP Negeri 6 Sungai Penuh, *Jurnal Program Studi Biologi Program Pascasarjana Universitas Negeri Padang*, v. 2, n. 2, 10-22.

Ezejitu, P. 2009. *Effect of cooperative learning on the achievement of secondary school students in Biology*. Unpublished BSc Ed thesis, Abakaliki; Department of Science Education, Ebonyi State University.

Fazio, X., Melville, W., & Bartley, A. 2010. The problematic nature of the practicum: A key determinant of preservice teachers' emerging Inquiry-based science practices. *Journal of Science Teacher Education, 21*(6), 665-681. doi:10.1007/s10972-010-9209-9.

Fraser, B. J. 1978. Development of a test of science related attitudes. *Science Education, 62*, 509-515.

Fraenkel, J. R., Wallen, N. E., & Hyun, H. H. 2012. *Internal validity. How to design and evaluate research in education*. New York: McGraw-Hill.

Folounrunso, B. E., & Sunday, A. O. 2017. Relative effectiveness of guided discovery and demonstration teaching techniques on students performance in Chemistry in senior secondary schools in Ile-Ife, Nigeria. *European Journal of Education Studies*, 3(9), 63–76.

Gallenstein, N. L. 2004. Creative discovery through classification (early childhood corner). *Teaching Children Mathematics*, 11, 103- 108.

Gerver, R. K. & Sgroi, R. J. 2003. Creating and using guided-discovery lessons. *Mathematics Teacher*, 96(1), 6-13.

George, R. 2006. A Cross-domain analysis of change in students' attitudes toward science and attitudes about the utility of science, *International Journal of Science Education*, Vol. 28, No. 6, 571–589.

Galadima, 1. 2003. Disparity between Expected and Actual Outcomes in the Nigerian Educational System. *Nigerian Journal of Curriculum Studies*, 10(2), 457–460.

Gijlers, H., de Jong, T. 2005. "The Relation between Prior Knowledge and Students' Collaborative Discovery Learning Processes." *Journal of Research in Science Teaching.* 42(3), 264-282.

Hancock, C., Kaput, J. J., & Goldsmith, L. T. 1992. Authentic inquiry with data: Critical baniers to classroom implementation. *Educational Psychologist*, 27, 337-364.

Hurd, P. D. 2000. Science education for the 21st century. *School Science and Mathematics.* 100(6), 282-289.

Hake, R. R. 2002. "Relationship of individual student normalized learning gains in mechanics with gender, high-school physics, and pretest scores on mathematics and spatial visualization," submitted to the *Physics Education Research Conference*; online at http://www.physics. indiana.edu/~hake/PERC2002h-Hake.pdf.

Hermann, R. S., & Miranda, R. J. 2010. A Template for Open Inquiry. *Science Teacher*, 77(8), 26-30.

Hofstein, A. & Lunetta, V. N. 2004. The laboratory in science education: foundations for the twenty-first century. *Science Education,* 88(1), 28-54.

Hoirina, Afifah N. & Dahlia. 2015. Analisis Aktivitas Belajar Biologi Siswadengan Menggunakan Media Gambar Kelas VII SMP Negeri 3 Rambah Samo Tahun Pembelajaran 2014/2015. *E-Journal Universitas Pasir Pengaraian.* 1(1): 332-338.

Ilahi, T M. 2012. *Pembela-jaran Discovery Strategy & MentalVocational Skill.* Jogjakarta: DIVA Press.

Inoue, N., & Buczynski, S. 2010. You Asked Open-Ended Questions, Now What? Understanding the Nature of Stumbling Blocks in Teaching Inquiry Lessons. *Mathematics Educator,* 20(2), 10-23.

Işık, A. D. 2007. *The Effects of Learning Package Prepared According to the Constructivist Approach on Information Technologies Course.* Unpublished Master Thesis, Dokuz Eylül University, İzmir.

Jacobsen, David A. Paul Eggen & Donald Kauchak, 2009. *Methods for Teaching, Terjemahan oleh Achmad Fawaid dan Khoirul Uman*, Yogyakarta: Pustaka Pelajar.

Koç, A. & Böyük, U. 2012. The Effect of Hands-on Science Experiments on Attitude towards Science. *Journal of Turkish Science Education, 9* (4), 102-118.

Lee, J. J. 2004. *Taiwanese student's scientific attitudes, environmental perceptions, self-efficacy and achievement in microbiology courses. Doctoral Dissertation.* The University of South Dakota.

Li, Q., Moorman, L. & Dyjur, P. 2010. Inquiry-based learning and e-mentoring via videoconference: a study of mathematics and science learning of Canadian rural students. *Educational Technology Research and Development,* 58(6), 729-753. 10.1007/s11423-010-9156-3.

Liu, O., Lee, H., & Linn, M. 2010. An investigation of teacher impact on student inquiry science performance using a hierarchical linear model. *Journal of Research in Science Teaching*, 47, 807–819. doi:10. 1002/tea.20372.

Luera, G., Killu, K., & O'Hagen, J. 2003. Linking math, science, and inquiry-based learning: An example from a mini-unit on volume. *School Science and Mathematics*, 103(4), 194-207.

Lynch, J. 1986. *Multicultural education: Principles and practices.* London, UK: Routledge and Kegan Paul.

Mahlail, F. I., Susilowati, S. M. E. & Anggraito, Y. U. 2018. Developing Guided Discovery Based Biology Teaching Material Supported by Pictorial Analysis, *Journal of Innovative Science Education*, 7(1), 25-35.

Majid, A. 2008. *Perencanaan Pembelajaran: Mengembangkan Standar Kompetensi Guru.* Bandung: PT. Remaja Rosdakarya.

Marriott, C. E. 2014. Just wondering. *Knowledge Quest,* 43(2), 74-76.

Marshall, J., & Horton, R. 2011. The relationship of teacher-facilitated, inquiry-based instruction to student higher-order thinking. *School Science and Mathematics*, 111. http://www.freepatentsonline.com/art icle/SchoolScienceMathematics/250321509.html.

Martins, O. O. and Oyebanji, R. K. 2000. Theeffects of inquiry and lecture teaching approaches on the cognitive achievement of integrated science students. *Journal of Science Teachers' Association of Nigeria.* 35 (1&2) 25-30.

Mattern, N., & Schau, C. 2002. Gender differences in science attitude–achievement relationships over time among white middle-school students. *Journal of Research in Science Teaching,* 39, 324–340.

Matthews, M. R. 2002. Constructivism and Science Education: A Further Appraisal, *Journal of Science Education and Technology,* Vol. 11, No. 2, 121-134.

MoNE (Ministry of National Education). 2003. *Elementary Science and Technology Education Curriculum.* Ankara.

MoNE. 2016. *Elementary Science Education Curriculum.* Ankara.

MoNE. 2017. *Elementary Science Education Curriculum.* Ankara.

Minner, D. D., Levy, A. J., & Century, J. 2010. Inquiry-based science instruction— What is it and does it matter? Results from a research synthesis years 1984–2002. *Journal of Research in Science Teaching,* 47, 474–496. doi:10.1002/tea.20347.

Mukherjee, A. 2015. Effective Use of Discovery Learning to Improve Understanding of Factors That Affect Quality. *Journal of Education for Business.* 90: 413–419.

Nasution, S. 2009. Berbagai Pendekatan dalam Proses Belajar dan Mengajar [*Various Approaches in Learning and Teaching*]. Jakarta: Bumi Aksara.

Njoku, Z. C. 2004. Fostering the application of science education research findings in Nigeria classrooms: Strategies and needs development. In M. A. G. Akale (Ed.) *45th Annual conference proceedings of Science Teachers Association of Nigeria (pp 217-222):* Ibadan; Heinemann Educational Books Limited.

Novak, J. D. & Canas, A. J. 2009. *The development and evolution of the concept mapping tool leading to a new model for mathematics education.* K. Afamasaga-Fuata'i (Ed.), Concept Mapping in Mathematics: Research into Practice. Ny: Springer.

Omiko, A. 2016. An Evaluation of Classroom Experiences of Basic Science Teachers in Secondary Schools in Ebonyi State of Nigeria. *British Journal of Education,* Vol. 4, No. 1, pp. 64-76.

Otobo, K. 2012. *Effect of Guided Discovery method of instruction on the achievement of junior secondary school students in computer studies,*

Abakaliki. Unpublished BScEd degree thesis. Department of science, Ebonyi State University.

Özay, E., Ocak, İ. & Ocak, G. 2003. The Effect of Gender on the Academic Achievement and Retention in General Biology Practice. *Journal of Pamukkale Universtiy Education Faculty*, 2(14): 63-67.

Krisnawati, E. 2015. *The Implementation of Teaching Writing Using Discovery Learning to the Eighth Grade Students at SMPN 1 Grogol in Academic Year 2014/2015.* Unpublished Thesis: English Department, University of Nusantara PGRI Kediri.

Parker, V., & Gerber, B. 2000. Effects of a science intervention program on middle grade student achievement and attitudes. *School Science and Mathematics*, 100(5), 236–242.

Pehlivan, H., & Köseoğlu, P. 2010. The Reliability and Validity Study of the Attitude Scale for Biology Course. *Procedia-Social and Behavioral Sciences*, 2, 2185-2188.

Preece, P. F. W. & Brotherton, P. N. 1997. Teaching Science Process Skills: Long-Term Effects on Science Achievement. International *Journal of Science Education*, 19(8), 895-901.

Ristiono, R., Novriyanti, E. & Yudha, L. T. 2012. Pengaruh Penggunaan Media *Puzzle* Gambar Berwarna dalam Pembelajaran Kooperatif Tipe NHT terhadap Hasil Belajar Biologi Siswa Kelas XI Sman 1 Koto XI Tarusan. *Ta'dib*. 15(1):105-109.

Safitri, D., Zubaidah, S., & Gofur, A. 2014. Pengembangan Bahan Ajar Mata Kuliah Biologi Sel pada Program Studi Pendidikan Biologi Di Universitas Nusantara PGRI Kediri. *Bioedukasi*. 7(2):47-52.

Safryadi, A. 2016. Pembelajaran Biologi Pokok Bahasan Sistem Pernapasanpada Manusia Melalui Media Gambardi MTs NJongarankabupaten Aceh Tenggara. *Jurnal Biotik*. 4(2):143-148.

Saka, A. Z. 2004. Concretization Tools and Application Levels Used In Science Teaching. IV. National Congress of Science and Matematics Education, v. 1, pp. 245, İstanbul.

Schauble, L., Glaser, R., Duschl, R. A., Schulze, S., & John, J. 1995. Students' understanding of the objectives and procedures of experimentation in the science classroom. *The Journal of the Learning Sciences*, 4, 131-166.

Sembiring, S. A., & Sihombing E. 2014. Penerapan Model Pembelajaran Guided Discovery untuk Meningkatkan Hasil Belajar Siswa pada Materi Pokok Suhu dan Kalor di Kelas X Semester II SMA Negeri 1 Kuala T. A. 2012/2013. *Inpafi.* 2(4): 146-153.

Silva, R. M., 2000. *Didactic Texts: Criticismand Expectations.* 1st Edn., Alínea, ISBN: 8586491640, pp: 154.

Singer, J. E., Krajcik, J. S., Marx, R. W., & Clay-Chambers, J. 2000. Constructing extended inquiry projects: Curriculum materials for science education reform. *Educational Psychologist*, 35(3), 165–179.

Sönmez, E., Dilber, R., Alver, B., Aksakallı, A. & Karaman. İ. 2006. An Investigatian Towards Important or the Instruction Technology and Material Development Lesson. *Journal of Kazım Karabekir Education Faculty.* v. 3, 113-119.

Sungur, S. & Tekkaya, C. 2003. Students' Achievement in Human Circular System Unit: The Effects of Reasoning Ability and Gender, *Journal of Science Education and Technology*, 12, 59-64.

Slavin, R. E. 1994. *A Practical Guide to Cooperative Learning.* Needham Heights, MA: Allyn and Bacon.

Şengül, N. 2006. *The Effect of Active Teaching Methods Based on Constructivism Theory on Students' Achievement and Attitudes about Flowing Electricity.* Master Thesis. University of Celal Bayar. Manisa.

Şenler, B. 2014. Turkish Adaptation of the Competence Scale for Learning Science: Validity and Reliability Study. *Journal of Theory and Practice in Education, 10*(2): 393-407 ISSN: 1304-9496.

Tal, T., Krajcik, J., & Blumenfeld, P. 2006. Urban schools' teachers enacting project-based science. *Journal of Research in Science Teaching*, 43(7), 722–745.

Taraban, R., Box, C., Myers, R., Pollard, R., & Bowen, C. W. 2007. Effects of Active-Learning Experiences on Achievement, Attitudes, and Behaviors in High School Biology. *J. Res. Sci. Teach.* 44(7): 960-979.

Teker, S., Kurt, M. & Karamustafaoğlu, O. 2017. The Effect of Students' Attitude and Success of "Propagation of Light and Sound" Unit through Discovery Learning. *Journal of Adıyaman University Social Institute*. v. 10.

Thair, M. & Treagust, D. F. 1997. A Review of Teacher Development Reforms in Indonesian Secondary Science: The Effectiveness of Practical Work in Biology, *Research in Science Education*, 27(4), 581–597

Tran, T., Nguyen, N. G., Bui, M. D. & Phan, A. H. 2014. Discovery Learning with the Help of the GeoGebra Dynamic Geometry Software, *International Journal of Learning, Teaching and Educational Research,* Vol. 7, No. 1, pp. 44-57.

Treagust, D. F., Chittleborough, G. & Mamiala, T. L. 2002. Students' Understanding of the Role of Scientific Models in Learning Science. *International Journal of Science Education, 24*, 4, 357–368.

Tretter, T., & Jones, M. 2003. *"Relationships between InquiryBased Teaching and Physical Science Standardized Test Scores,"* School Science and Mathematics Association, Vol. 103, No. 7, p. 345.

Udo, M. E. 2010. Effect of Guided-Discovery, Student- Centered Demonstration and the Expository Instructional Strategies on Students' Performance in Chemistry. An *International Multi-Disciplinary Journal.* 4(4):389-398.

Udo, M. E. & Udo, N. J. 2007. Instructional methods and the performance of students with different reasoning abilities in chemistry. *International Journal of Educational Development (IJED), 10*(1), 52-61.

Ünal, Ç. & Çelikkaya, T. 2009. The Effect of Constructive Approach on Success, Attitude and Permanency at the Social Sciences Teaching (5th Class Example). *Journal of Atatürk University Social Institute,* 13(2), 197-212.

Vellom, R. P., & Anderson, C. W. 1999. Reasoning About Data in Middle School Science. *Journal of Research in Science Teaching*, 36(2), 179 – 199.

Widiadnyana, I. W., Sadia I. W., & Suastra I. W. 2014. Pengaruh Model Discovery Learning Terhadap Pemahaman KonsepIPA dan SikapIlmiah Siswa SMP, *e-Journal Program Pascasarjana Universitas Pendidikan Ganesha Program Studi IPA*, v. 4.

Wulanzani, U. T., Lestari, U., & Syamsuri, I. 2016. Hasil Validasi Buku Teks Matakuliah Bioteknologi Berbasis Bahan Alam Tanaman Pacing (Costus Speciosus Smith) sebagai Antifertilitas [*Validation Results of Biotechnology Textbooks Based on Natural Plant Pacing (Costus Speciosus Smith) as Antifertility*]. *Jurnal Pendidikan: Teori, Penelitian, dan Pengembangan.* 1(9): 1830-1835.

Yiğit, N. & Akdeniz, A. R. 2003. The Effect of Computer-assisted Activities on Student Achievement in Physics Course: Electric Circuits Sample, *Journal of Gazi Education Faculty. v: 23*, no: 3, pp. 99-133.

Zint, M. 2002. Comparing Three Attitude–Behaviour Theories for Predicting Science Teachers' Intention. *Journal of Research in Science Teaching, 39* (9), 819–844.

In: Science Teaching and Learning ISBN: 978-1-53617-406-9
Editor: Paul J. Hendricks © 2020 Nova Science Publishers, Inc.

Chapter 5

AN INTEGRATED NOS MAP ON NATURE OF SCIENCE BASED ON THE PHILOSOPHY OF SCIENCE, AND THE DIMENSIONS OF LEARNING IN SCIENCE

Jun-Young Oh[1,2,], Yeon-A Son[3] and Norman G. Lederman[4]*

[1]Professor, Hanyang University,
Seoul 04763, Republic of Korea
[2]Institute for Education of Integrated Science, Dankook University,
Jukjeon 16890, Republic of Korea
[3]Professor, Department of Science Education, College of Education,
Dankook University, Jukjeon 16890, Republic of Korea
[4]Professor. Department of Mathematics and Science Education
Illinois Institute of Technology, Chicago, IL 60616, USA

ABSTRACT

The aims of this research are, (i) to consider Kuhn's concept of how scientific revolution takes place based on individual elements or

---

[*] Corresponding Author's Email: jyoh3324@hanyang.ac.kr.

tenets of Nature of Science (NOS), and (ii) to explore the inter-relationships within the individual elements or tenets of nature of science (NOS), based on the dimensions of scientific knowledge in science learning, this study suggests that instruction according to our Explicit Integrated NOS Map should include the tenets of NOS. The aspects of NOS that have been emphasized in recent science education reform documents disagree with the received views of common science. Additionally, it is valuable to introduce students at the primary level to some of the ideas developed by Kuhn. Key aspects of NOS are, in fact, good applications to the history of science through Kuhn's philosophy. Therefore, an Explicit Integrated NOS Flow Map could be a promising means of understanding the NOS tenets and an explicit and reflective tool for science teachers to enhance scientific teaching and learning.

Keywords: nature of science, integrated NOS flow map, attitudes, skills, knowledge, scientific literacy, Kuhn's philosophy

INTRODUCTION

In the past few years, the role of nature of science (NOS) in supporting scientific literacy has become widely institutionalized in curriculum standards internationally (Allchin, 2014). Understanding NOS is a central component of scientific literacy (AAAS, 1990; Lederman, Abd-El-Khalick, Bell, & Schwartz, 2002) and a central tenet in science education reform (NRC, 1996). Because scientific literacy involves an understanding of NOS, it is assumed that one will achieve scientific literacy if one obtains a fuller understanding of NOS (Meichtry, 1992; NRC, 1996). Rather than being memorized, however, NOS is experienced; and when we experience NOS, we achieve enhanced scientific literacy. Thus, the scientific enterprise is composed of at least two parts—processes and products—which involve attitudes as well as facts, theories, laws, and applications as a result of doing science (Martin, 2012, p. 40). NOS requires assumptions involving knowledge products (McComas et al., 1998, p. 4); thus, NOS involves understanding the limits of the scientific method, the nature of scientific knowledge, and the historical situations of their developments (Lederman et al., 1992, 1999).

Despite continuing disagreements about a specific definition for NOS, at a certain level of generality and within a certain period of time (Allchin, 2011; Allchin, 2012), those aspects of NOS that are of interest for this study are generally agreed on (Martin, 2012; Akerson et al., 2010; Akerson et al., 2007; Lederman, 2006; Lederman et al., 2002). As summarized by Lederman and his colleagues (Lederman et al., 2002), these aspects are as follows:

Scientific knowledge is tentative (subject to change), empirically based (based on and/or derived from observations of the natural world), and subjective (involves the personal background, biases, and/or is theory-laden); necessarily involves human inference, imagination, and creativity (involves the invention of explanations); and is socially and cultural embedded. Two additional important aspects are the distinction between observation and inferences, and the functions of and relationships between theories and laws (p. 499).

Abd-El-Khalick et al., (2008) subdivided NOS into 10 different features, in which social dimensions are separated from social and cultural embeddedness. Within this framework, social dimensions and cultural embeddedness are combined into one feature for this research. Practically, we constructed an NOS Flow Map and applied it to the evolution of the structure of the atom. Because we limited our discussion to Kuhn, we look at what cognitive science has to say about how individuals learn science (Carey, 2009; Clement, 2008; Nersessian, 2008) and show the parallels in how novel scientific knowledge develops, especially demonstrating how individuals (novices and experts alike) succumb to the same pressures. We offer examples from science history that provide explicit ways to reflect about this connection. This approach may help students be more aware of their own learning and empower them to take some ownership in it.

While teachers must accurately understand the history, philosophy, and sociology of science in order to accurately teach the NOS, such understanding as well as science content understanding does not ensure effective instruction. Research makes clear that students' attention must be overtly drawn to NOS ideas in a manner that requires them to mentally engage and wrestle with those issues (Clough, 2018). Thus, we claim that other factors, Integrated strategies about tenets of NOS, are also important.

Purpose

This research aims to explore, the procedure scientific revolution as defined by Kuhn, in order to explore the development of scientific knowledge in the history of science, the inter-relationship among the individual elements or tenets of the NOS in the context of the dimensions of scientific knowledge in science learning, and how it applies to the Einstein's special theory of relativity of, one of the modern sciences. It is included in the physics curriculum of high school in South Korea, but it is very difficult to learn it because it is not related to the historical process.

Firstly, we will investigate how Kuhn's philosophy and history of science are connected with NOS. Here, we must look at Kuhn's emphasis on scientific work as essentially communal and social because natural science also has a social character: namely, the scientific community.

Second, we will explore the comprehensive viewpoints by exploring the dimensions of learning in science: Knowledge, Skills, and Attitudes in nature of science.

METHODS

Kuhn's Scientific Revolution for the Tenets of NOS

This section explains the social and cultural embeddedness and social dimension of scientific knowledge and the crisis of normal science as Kuhn explained it. Using a flowchart, which is a tool for simplification, also has some restrictions in that a Kuhnian revolution may be only one way to consider the process of science. However, as Eflin, Glennan, and Reisch (1999) observe,

It is valuable to introduce students at an elementary level to some of the ideas developed by Kuhn. In particular, students benefit by considering the idea that different paradigms compete with each other, and that they can easily understand some of the ways in which theoretical commitments and social issues can influence the development of science. On the other hand, students should be made aware that some interpretations of Kuhn's views are extreme and not persuasive (radical incommensurability) (p. 114).

We turn now to examining the steps or stages in Kuhn's concept of a scientific revolution. *A crisis in normal science* occurs as a result of a number of serious anomalies. In the case of Copernicus, scientists have formulated several elaborate and differing story lines about the heliocentric hypothesis at the time of Copernicus. The dominant problems centered on "calendar reform" and "complexity" in explaining the heavens (Charmers, 1999, p. 113). Kuhn described episodes of theory change as tumultuous periods during which scientists with established venues for communication and criticism judged competing theories using a variety of criteria, including social influences (Sadler, 2004). Also, preparing students to achieve the lofty goal of functional scientific literacy entails addressing the normative and non-normative facets of socio-scientific issue (SSI), such as scientific processes, nature of science (NOS) and diverse sociocultural perspectives (Herman, 2018). Thus we claim that SSI, along with diverse sociocultural perspectives, is the most important elements of NOS tenets.

The seriousness of the crisis in normal science then deepens as a result of the appearance of an alternative. *Subjectivity* enters at this stage, for although the crisis in the paradigm is recognized in terms of a socio-cultural need and the problem is partially solved by the submission of new alternatives, new problems are posed with the new paradigm. However, for the disciplinary successors of the new paradigm, new alternatives emerge as the severity of the crisis intensifies for the paradigm. In other words, study is begun to solve the new problems. The subjective and theory-dependent empirical data indicate the study direction of the new paradigm. One of Kuhn's ideas about the nature of science is the *theory-ladenness of observations.* In ancient Greece, Aristarchus suggested that the earth may rotate on its axis and revolve in an orbit around the sun. Almost 2000 years later, Copernicus also came to a conclusion about the system of the universe based on the combination of the earth's two motions about the Sun. In particular, he could explain the retrograde motions of planets without the complex epicycles suggested by Ptolemy (Cohen, 1985, p. 45).

The Copernican system has more problems in the observational sense than the Ptolemaic system, because Aristotle's idea of the celestial bodies accepted the notion of the uniform circular motion in what is called a natural motion. However, it strongly attracted such disciplinary successors as Galileo, Kepler, and Newton because of its beauty. In other words, Neo-Platonism, which was popular at that time, emphasized simplicity and beauty (qualitatively simple and harmonious), whereas the Ptolemaic system tried to explain in a more and more complicated way. Theory-ladenness relates to social and cultural changes, as well as subjectivity. In terms of accuracy, Ptolemy's model is better than Copernicus's model. As well, Neo-Platonism is based on a certain degree of comprehension, not just simplicity. "Putting the Earth in motion around the Sun was that it immediately suggested that Copernicus had not just a workable astronomy but a seemingly coherent cosmology" (Henry, 2012, p. 71).

A scientific revolution is then completed by disciplinary successors who follow a new paradigm. Science's necessary reliance on empirical evidence is what distinguishes it from other disciplines (e.g., religion, philosophy). Although this evidence may be explained by the new theory, new evidence will still be predicted and estimated. *Empirical Evidence* supporting Copernicus's heliocentric hypothesis. Given the empirical evidence for Copernicus's heliocentric theory, mathematical abstraction and idealization in thought experiences became very important in Galileo's research, especially in the study of dynamics. Galileo demonstrated that *inference* is very important, beyond accurate observation on natural phenomena. *Empirical data* that have a favorable influence upon Newton's theory.

Observations and Inference

Based on the observations of Tycho Brahe, Kepler was able to discard the annoying epicycles with a planet's elliptical orbit rather than a circular orbit. Kepler's inference is more significant than Brahe's because he could not estimate an elliptical orbit directly from Tycho Brahe's data. Rather, he explained Brahe's observations because he thought of an elliptical orbit through an intermediate form from an initial circular orbit.

An accurate elliptical orbit is difficult to derive from observation because an accurate elliptical orbit revolves only when there is only one planet with a sun of infinite mass. Thus, the abstraction work of inference is required. Therefore, rather than estimating scientific empirical data from simple observations, inference is absolutely necessary, and this requires a scientist's creativity. Moreover, not only is inference required to interpret observation data but also it becomes the foundation of predicting further observation data.

Law and theory are both in the so-called "hierarchy of credibility," found in most science textbooks, which presents categories of scientific knowledge/ideas (i.e., observations, hypotheses, theories, laws/principles) in an ascending list of credibility or certainty. Individuals often hold the common sense, hierarchical view of the relationship between theories and laws presented in such lists. In this view, theories become laws as they accumulate supporting evidence over numerous years. It follows from this notion that scientific laws have a higher status than scientific theories.

The common notions relating to theories and laws are inappropriate because, among other things, theories and laws are different kinds of knowledge and the one cannot develop or be transformed into the other. Laws are *statements or descriptions of the relationships* among observable phenomena. Theories, by contrast, *are inferred explanations* for observable phenomena.

No Universal Step by Step Scientific Method, Individual Creativity

The development of scientific knowledge is based partly on human *imagination and creativity*. Scientific knowledge is not simply the product of logic and rationality. Scientists follow many and various methods in order to produce scientific knowledge (AAAS, 1993; NRC, 1996: Shapin, 1996). Throughout scientific history, diverse disciplinary successors have not constructed certain laws or theories by a simple collection of data and logical induction; rather, their work has been pursued creatively through insight to solve the problems inherent in a new paradigm.

Law and Theory

Newton's most significant contribution was the law of the universal gravitation, and by this theory, Newton could explain Kepler's law of planetary motion and Galileo's law of falling.

The stage of the new Normal Science and Its Recycling (Expansion)

Tentative Character of Scientific Theory

In Newton's theory system, the celestial and terrestrial worlds are unified as one, and each object moves with the force of Newton's law of motion. As soon as Newton's physics was constructed, it was applied in detail to astronomy. However, the discrepancy of Newton's mechanics with electromagnetism and the explanation of Mercury's perihelion shifting provided an opportunity for Einstein to construct his new theory of relativity.

In sum, scientific knowledge is a product of recycling the revolution process toward discovery of a new philosophy and theory system as well as an accumulation procedure through revision and development. Therefore, conflicting ideas may arise from various interpretations of the same data based on individual theory.

As shown in Table 1, 'the Social and Cultural effects, & Social dimension' shown in the bottom part of Figure 1 correspond to 'Kuhn's A crisis in normal science'. The yellow area of the process of inquiry corresponds to 'the seriousness of a crisis of Kuhn' and 'the revolution completion by disciplinary successors of a new paradigm'. However,' theory-ladenness, of subjective in tenets of NOS', is commonly associated with Kuhn's 'A crisis in normal science and seriousness of a crisis.' The yellow area is the products of the inquiry process and is the result of 'Kuhn's Revolution Completion by disciplinary successors of a new paradigm.'

An Integrated NOS Map in Nature of Science ...

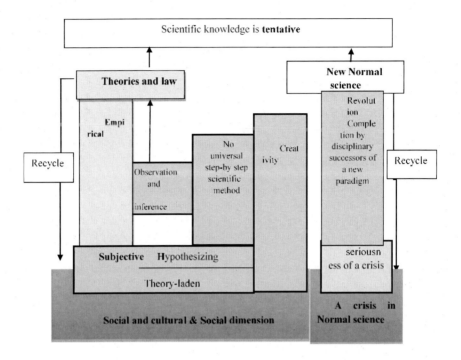

Figure 1. Relationship between tents of NOS and Kuhn's Scientific Revolution.

The Dimensions of Learning in Science: Knowledge, Skills, and Attitudes for the Tenets of NOS

Zeitler and Baruffaldi (1988) encourage educators to use the experience of scientific enquiries, scientific attitude, and basic scientific knowledge in teaching, which are all integrated as scientific literacy. Therefore, in this study it is necessary to present NOS as a combination of these three elements as well.

Attitudes about science can have a significant effect on scientific literacy. In *education theory*, understanding of content lies in the cognitive domain, while attitudes lie in the affective domain. According to Flick (1993), there are three major dimensions of learning in science: knowledge, skills, and attitudes.

The *knowledge dimension* of learning in science includes understanding of NOS and technology, science content, and unifying themes or concepts. Through skill activities, students can learn about NOS and technology as parallel human endeavors to create explanations for natural phenomena (science) and solve problems of human adaptation to the environment (technology) (Bybee, et al., 1989).

The skills dimension of learning includes bodily kinesthetic skills (gross, find motor, and eye-hand coordination) as well as training of the senses. Students can also learn skills in science processes such as inference, data analysis, and hypothesizing (AAAS, 1967) and general organizing skills such as information gathering, problem-solving, and decision making (Bybee, et al., 1989). Cooperative group arrangements and the need to interact with a variety of new materials provide opportunities for students to develop social (interpersonal) skills as well as intrapersonal and meta-cognitive awareness skills.

In the science education community, the rational or epistemological characteristics of science are typically tied to empiricism, the process of inquiry, differences between inference and observation, and the tentative nature of scientific conclusions (Abd-El-Khalick, 2012; Irzik & Nola, 2014; Lederman et al., 2006).

The *attitudes dimension* of learning includes attitudes of science. Attitudes of science are those habits of mind cultivated by scientific investigators for maintaining the integrity of the inquiry and the validity of the information. These include attitudes such as being skeptical, relying on data, and accepting ambiguity (Bybee, et al., 1989). As well as exploration of effects of SSI engagement on students' interest and motivation, some researchers have focused on the effects of Science-Technology-Society (STS) issues on students' attitudes towards science (Sadler, 2004). Yager et al., (2006) used an STS issue for one class and compared this class with a class following the standard middle school science curriculum. The attitude of students in the intervention class was found to be higher than in the comparison class. Lee and Erdogan (2007) conducted another STS engagement study for middle and high school students and found similar results with Yager et al.,'s (2006) findings that students developed positive attitudes towards science. However, SSI (socio-scientific issues) are different from the science issues in that they do not only focus on science content but also on social dimensions of this science content. An SSI approach is characterized by a reconceptualization of the STS approach, and it focuses on not only social dimensions of science and technology but also on students.

Although STS education emphasizes the impact of science and technology, there is also a view that ethical issues and students' moral development are not precisely focused (Zeidler et al., 2002). The importance of science-related social and ethical issues (Socioscientific issues, SSI) education, which includes the educational implications of STS and considers the ethical aspects of science and the morality and development of students, has also increased (Zeidler et al., 2002).

A "consensus view" (Erduran & Dagher, 2014, p. 5) of NOS emerged recently in science education research that describes social dimensions as including the theory-laden nature of scientific knowledge, creativity, and social and cultural embeddedness (Abd- El-Khalick, 2012; Lederman et al., 2002). Within this framework, social dimensions and cultural embeddedness are collapsed into one feature and separated from other attributes.

In this research, the theory-based nature of scientific knowledge is involved in the exchange of skill and attitude. But creativity is involved in skill detention rather than altitude dimension, we describe that the two "constantly interact with each other."

Martin (2012, p. 40) defined science as a process by which knowledge is produced. Thus, the scientific enterprise comprises at least two factors—processes and products. The products of science include the facts, concepts, theories, laws, and applications and attitudes that occur as a result of doing science. Zeitler and Barufaldi (1988, p. 10) defined scientific literacy as the melding of scientific investigative experience, attitudes, and basic knowledge. Therefore, acquiring scientific literacy should be well coordinated between a basic knowledge of science and experiential exploration and attitudes toward science. One development in this regard is the establishment of Project 2061, a publication consisting of a set of recommendations "spelling out the knowledge, skills, and attitudes all students should acquire as a consequence of their total science experience "(AAAS, 1989, p. 3) in order to be regarded as scientifically literate (Laugksch, 2000).

Martin (2012, p. 57) has described 'attitudes' as another scientific product, different from facts, concepts, generalization, theories, laws, and applications. These attitudes are formed by individual experiences and explorations; in turn, they affect our learning with explorations, which are once again affected by these attitudes.

In this research, the following terms are used for the processes of science learning that consist of attitude, skill, and knowledge: *Scientific attitudes* refer to the social dimension, social and cultural changes, and subjectivity (theory-ladenness). *Scientific skills* do not refer to specific scientific methods but rather to imagination and creativity, observation and inference, and subjectivity (hypothesizing). *Scientific knowledge* refers to law and theories, and the elements of nature of science the NOS necessary to achieve wider scientific literacy. In particular, subjectivity consists of hypothesizing (Skills, AAAS, 1967), and theory-ladenness (Attitudes, Martin, 2012).

In this study, the dimensions of science learning in science should be understood as supporting the tenet that scientific knowledge is tentative and revisionary.

A "consensus view" (Erduran & Dagher, 2014, p. 5) of NOS has emerged recently in science education research that describes the social dimension as including the theory-laden nature of scientific knowledge, creativity, and social and cultural embeddedness (Abd-El-Khalick, 2012; Lederman et al., 2002). Within this framework, social dimensions and cultural embeddedness are collapsed into one feature and separated from other attributes in this research, whereas the schema used by Abd-El-Khalick et al., (2008) subdivides NOS into 10 different features, in which social dimensions are separated from social and cultural embeddedness. Longino (2002) described social dimensions as including "constitutive values associated with established venues for communication and criticism within the scientific enterprise which serve to enhance the objectivity of collectively scrutinized scientific knowledge" (Abd-El-Khalick et al., 2008, p. 838), within intrinsic effects. The social and cultural aspects of NOS are described as processes by which scientific knowledge claims are "affected by their social and historical milieu" (Niaz & Maza, 2011) or "embedded and practiced in the context of a larger cultural milieu" (Abd-El-Khalick et al., 2008, p. 839), within extrinsic effects.

One important aspect of science is the *observation* of events. However, observation requires *imagination and creativity*, for scientists can never include everything in a description of what they observe. Hence, scientists must make judgments about what is relevant in their observations. Empirical theory would argue that there is no imagination and creativity in observation because it happens automatically, though it is filtered by the senses and brain. It is the *interpretation* of those records in our brain, the empiricist would say, that relies on creativity and imagination.

The role of *creativity and imagination* in the development of scientific knowledge also has implications for the supposed objectivity of science; even so-called "objective facts" in science are not really free from *subjectivity*. Scientists' backgrounds, theoretical and disciplinary commitments, and expectations all strongly influence their work. These factors produce a mindset that affects what scientists investigate, how they conduct their investigations, and how they interpret their observations. As two prominent examples, Aristotle (384-322 B.C.) and Galileo (1564-1642) both interpreted motion along a horizontal surface. Aristotle noted that objects, after an initial push, always slow down and stop. Consequently, he believed that the natural state of an object is to be at rest, supporting the geocentric hypothesis that, in his social and cultural context, distinguished between the celestial world and the terrestrial world. Galileo imagined that if friction could be eliminated, an object given an initial push along a horizontal surface would continue to move indefinitely without stopping. He concluded it was just as natural for an object to be in motion as to be at rest. He did so with a leap of the imagination. Galileo made this leap conceptually without actually eliminating friction, supporting the heliocentric hypothesis that unified the celestial and terrestrial worlds' laws, based on the simplicity of Neo-Platonism.

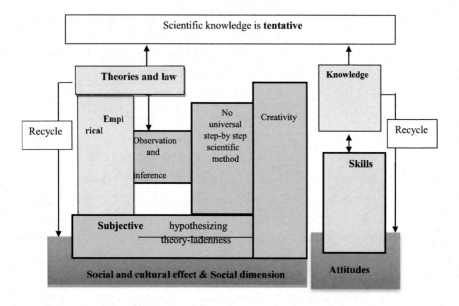

Figure 2. The tenets of NOS and the dimensions of learning in science.

These two examples demonstrate the *distinction between observations and inference,* which is significant in science because these two types of scientific knowledge give rise to different kinds of scientific claims. The *laws* express a relationship that can describe what happens under specific conditions, but *scientific theories* offer explanations for why something happens. Additionally, because both laws and theories are based on tentative knowledge (observation and inferences), neither is absolute. When considering its empirical nature, it is important to remember that scientific knowledge is a product of *both observation and inference.* Observations constitute the empirical basis of scientific knowledge: they are descriptions of natural phenomena that may be directly perceived by the senses (or instrumental extensions of the senses). Inferences are conjectures beyond observable data. The distinction between observations and inferences in science is significant because these two types of scientific knowledge give rise to different kinds of scientific claims. Science involves more than the accumulation of countless observations—rather, it is derived from a combination of observation and explanations derived from observations, and it often involves entities that are not directly observable.

Bauer (1994) said that scientific knowledge is composed of the following: fundamental concepts in science, the nature of scientific activities, and the role of science in society-culture. One who achieves these three types of knowledge is a person well-equipped with scientific literacy. In light of these elements, scientific literacy is actually a part of historical and cultural literacy. Anyone who understands that scientific progress is limited through a filter of scientific agreement can develop their science literacy, even if he or she does not know the content of science very well. Accordingly, our research ranks these scientists, socio-cultural contexts, and attitudes as foundational in terms of affecting the development of scientific knowledge.

Table 1. The views about the elements of NOS

	The elements of NOS		
Scientific Literacy (Zeitler & Barufaldi, 1988)	**Skill**	**Attitude**	**Knowledge**
Inter-relationship NOS	Process of inquiry	Social dimension	Productions
	No scientific methods, observation & inference (theory –dependence, creativity)	Social and Cultural effects, & Social dimension (theory –ladenness, creativity)	Scientific knowledge, Empirical
Kuhn's Philosophy and History of Science	The seriousness of a crisis & Revolution Completion by disciplinary successors of a new paradigm	A crisis in Normal science	Revolution Completion by disciplinary successors of a new paradigm

As shown in Table 1, 'the Social and Cultural effects, & Social dimension', shown in the bottom area of Figure 2, correspond to the 'Attitude of Scientific Literacy.' The yellow area of the process of inquiry corresponds to 'the skill of Scientific Literacy.' However, 'theory-ladenness' in the subjectivity NOS tenet, is commonly associated with the 'skill and attitude of Scientific Literacy.' The yellow area corresponds to the 'knowledge' of Scientific Literacy as products of the inquiry process.

DISCUSSION AND CONCLUSION

We insist that none of these aspects should be considered apart from the others. Thus, the key aspects of NOS should be viewed in this study as interdependent, dynamic, explicit, and reflective. Empiricists argue that our perception gives us objective facts about the world, configuring the foundations of science, and that general laws and theories are inductively produced, based on those facts. However, we maintain that judgments and inferences on observable facts in a specific situation will change depending on the person, the culture, and the theoretical school.

That is, under the themes of *social and cultural background,* including communication and criticism *(Social dimension)* within the scientific enterprise, perception is formed and developed in a decisive manner by the *subjectivity of observers,* which involves their cultural and theoretical background, expectations, and perspectives. Such considerations are handled under the heading of *the theory-ladenness of observation* in the philosophy of science. Additionally*, law,* which shows regularity, and *theory,* which requires our creativity, should be separated. We insist that *law* (regularity) and *theory* (creativity) should be considered as a dynamic combination rather than separated because of the theory-ladenness of observation. Likewise, most modern philosophers of science have questioned the hierarchical/dichotomous relationship between laws and theories (Giere, 1999; Nias & Maza, 2011, p. 5).

The development of scientific knowledge involves making observations about nature. That is, observations do not equate to *scientific methods,* which are represented as universal step-by-step processes. This additional aspect is what we have alluded to as "no single scientific method" but rather a host of methodologies to produce scientific knowledge (Lederman et al., 2002; Bell, 2006). Finally, because objective law or theory is not produced from objective facts, a scientific theory is, indeed, tentative. This research has proposed a new flow map, using core elements of NOS and the prerequisite conditions of a scientific revolution proposed by Kuhn (1996), to apply to the atomic understanding process.

The process of science learning is held to consist of attitudes, skills, and knowledge: *scientific attitudes* include social and cultural changes, and subjectivity (theory-ladenness; Martin, 2012), *scientific skills,* while involving no single scientific method, include imagination and creativity, observation and inference, and subjectivity (hypothesizing; AAAS, 1989); and *scientific knowledge* includes laws, theories, and empirical evidence. The elements or tenets of NOS necessary to achieve scientific literacy are connected with scientific content.

However, our explicit NOS approach instructions include the history and philosophy of science in a dynamic exchange with the history of science as focused on implicit NOS approach instruction. In this way, we can use historical case studies and encourage students to analyze for the multi-faceted effects of the direction of scientific knowledge creation (Allchin, 2013; Irzik & Nola, 2011; Osborne et al., 2003).

ACKNOWLEDGMENTS

This work was supported by the Ministry of Education of the Republic of Korea and the National Research Foundation of Korea (NRF-2017S1A5A2A01023529).

REFERENCES

Abd-El-Khalick, F. (2012). Nature of science in science education: Toward a coherent framework for synergistic research and development. In B. J. Fraser, K. Tobin, & C. McRobbie (Eds.), *Second international handbook of science education* (Vol. 2, pp. 1041 – 1060). Dordrecht, the Netherlands: Springer.

Abd-El-Khalick, F., Waters, M., & Le, A. (2008). Representations of nature of science in high school chemistry textbooks over the past four decades. *Journal of Research in Science Teaching*, 45(7), 835 – 855.

Akerson, V. L., Buzzelli, C. A. & Donnelly, L. A. (2010). One the Nature of Teaching nature of science: Pre-service early childhood teachers' instruction in preschool and elementary settings. *Journal of Research in Science Teaching*, 47(2), 213–233.

Akerson, V. L., Hanson, D. L. & Cullen, T. A. (2007). The influence of guided inquiry and eplicit instruction on K-6 teachers' views of nature of science. *Journal of Science Teacher Education,* 18(5), 751–772.

Allchin, D. (2011). Evaluating Knowledge of the Nature of (Whole) Science. *Science Education*, 95(3), 518-542.

Allchin, D. (2012). Towards clarity on Whole Science and KNOWS. *Science Education*, 96, 693-700.

Allchin, D. (2013). *Teaching the nature of science: Perspectives & resources*. Saint Paul, Minnesota: SHiPS Education Press.

Allchin, D. (2014). From Science Studies to Scientific Literacy: A View from the Classroom. *Science & Education, Online First.*

American Association for the Advancement of Science (AAAS). (1967). *Guide for inservice instruction.* Washington: AAAS Miscellaneous Publication.

American Association for the Advancement of Science. (AAAS) (1989). *Project 2061-Science for all Americans. Washington, DC: AAAS.*

American Association for the Advancement of Science. (AAAS) (1990). *Science for all Americans. New York: Oxford University Press.*

American Association for the Advancement of Science. (AAAS) (1993). *Benchmarks for science literacy: A Project 2061 report*. New York: Oxford University Press.

Bauer, H. H. (1994). *Scientific literacy and the myth of the scientific method*. Urbana and Chicago: University of Illinois Press.

Bell. R. L. (2006). Perusing Pandora's Box. In L. B. Flick and N. G. Lederman (Eds.), *Scientific Inquiry and Nature of Science (pp. 427-446)*. The Netherland: Springer.

Brown, J. R. (1991). *Thought Experiments: A Platonic Account, in Tamara Horowitz & Gerald Massey (eds.), Thought Experiments in Science and Philosophy*. Lanham: Rowman & Littlefield.

Brown, J. R. (2011). *The Laboratory of the Mind: Thought Experiments in the Natural Sciences (2nd Edition)*. London: Routledge.

Bybee, R. W., Buchwald, C. E., Crissman, S., Kuerbis, P. J., Matsumoto, C., and McInerney, J. D. (1989). *Science and technology education for the elementary school: framework for curriculum and instruction*. Andover, MA and Washington, DC: A Partnership of the NETWORK, Inc. and the Biological Sciences Curriculum Study, Colorado Springs, CO.

Carey, S. (2009). The origin of concepts. Oxford; New York: Oxford University Press.

Chalmers, A. F. (1999). *What is this thing called science? (3rd. edition)*. Cambridge: Hackett Publishing Company, Lnc.

Clement, J. J. (2008). Creative model construction in scientists and students: The role of imagery, analogy, and mental simulation. Dordercht: Springer. Clough, M. P. (2006). Learners' responses to the demands of conceptual change: considerations for effective nature of science instruction. *Science Education, 15*, 463–494.

Clough, M. P. (2018). Teaching and Learning About the Nature of Science. *Science & education*, 27, 1-5.

Cohen, I. B. (1985). *The Birth of a New Physics: Revised and Updated*. New York: W. W. Norton & Company, Inc.

Erduran, S., & Dagher, Z. (2014). *Reconceptualizing the nature of science for science education: Scientific knowledges, practices and other family categories.* Dordrecht, the Netherlands: Springer.

Eflin, J. T., Glennan, S., & Reisch, G. (1999). The nature of science: A perspective from the philosophy of science. *Journal of Research in Science Teaching,* 36(1), 107-116.

Flick, L. B. (1993). The meanings of hands-on science. *Journal of Science Teacher Education,* 4(1), 3-4.

Giere, R. N. (1999). *Science without laws.* Chicago: University of Chicago Press.

Gribanov, D. P. (1987). *The Einstein's Philosophical Views and the Theory of Relativity.* Moscow: Progress Publisher.

Halpern, P. (2004). The Great Beyond: High Dimensions, Parallel Universes, and the Extraordinary Search for a Theory of Everything. The Anderson Literacy Agency.

Henry, J. (2012). *A Short History of Scientific Thought.* UK: Palgrave Macmillan.

Herman, B. C. (2018). Students' environmental NOS views, compassion, intent, and action: Impact of place-based socio-scientific issues instruction. *Journal of Research in Science Teaching, 55,* 600-638.

Irzik, G., & Nola, R. (2014). New directions for nature of science research. In M. Matthews (Ed.), *International handbook of research in history, philosophy and science teaching* (pp. 999 – 1021). New York, NY: Springer.

Irzik, G., & Nola, R. (2011). A Family Resemblance Approach to the Nature of Science for Science Education. *Science & Education,* 20(7), 591-607.

Kuhn, T. S. (1996). *The Structure of Scientific revolutions (3rd Edition),* Chicago: The University of Chicago Press.

Laugksch, R. C. (2000). Scientific Literacy: A Conceptual Overview. *Science Education, 84,* 71-94.

Lee, M., and Erdogan, I. (2007). The effect of science-technology-society teaching on students' attitudes toward science and certain aspects of creativity. *International Journal of Science Education, 11,* 1315-1327.

Longino, H. (2002). *The fate of knowledge*. Princeton, NJ: Princeton University Press.

Lederman, N. G. (1992). Students' and teacher's conceptions of the nature of science: A review of the research. *Journal of Research in Science Teaching*, 29, 331-359.

Lederman, N. G. (2006). Syntax of Nature of Science within Inquiry and Science Instruction. In L. B. Flick, and N. G. Lederman (Eds.), *Scientific Inquiry and Nature of Science* (pp. 301-317). Netherland: Springer.

Lederman, N. G., Abd-El-Khalick, F., Bell, R. L., & Schwartz, R. S. (2002). Views of NOS questionnaire toward valid and meaningful assessment of learners' conceptions of NOS. *Journal of Research in Science Teaching,* 39, 497-521.

Martin, D. J. (2012). *Elementary Science Methods: A Constructivist Approach (6th Edition).* Canada: Wadsworth, Cengage Learning

McComas, W. F., Clough, M. P., and Almazroa, H. (1998). The role and character of the nature of science in science education. In W. F. McComas (ed.), *The role and character of the nature of science in science education: rationales and strategies (pp. 3-39).* New York: Kluwer Academic Publication.

Meichtry, Y. J. (1992). Influencing student understanding of the nature of science: Data from a case from curriculum development. *Journal of Research in Science Teaching*, 29(4), 389-407.

Miller, A. (1998). *Insights of Genius.* New York: Springer-Verlag.

National Research Council (NRC) (1996). *National science education standards. Washington.* DC: National Academic Press.

Nersessian, N. J. (2008). *Creating scientific concepts.* Cambridge, Mass.: MIT Press.

Niaz, M. & Maza, A. (2011). *Nature of Science in General Chemistry Textbooks.* New York: Springer.

Oh, J. Y. (2016). Understanding Galileo's dynamics through Free Falling Motion. *Foundations of Science, 21*(4), 567-578.

Oh, J.-Y. (2017). Suggesting a NOS Map for Nature of Science for Science Education Instruction. *Eurasia Journal of Mathematics Science and Technology Education, 13(5)*, 1461-1483.

Osborne, J., Collins, S., Ratcliffe, M., Millar, R., & Duschl, R. (2003). What "ideas-about-science" should be taught in school science? A Delphi study of the expert community. *Journal of Research in Science Teaching*, 40(7), 692-720.

Sadler, T. D. (2004). Informal Reasoning Regarding Socioscientific Issues: A Critical Review of Research. *Journal of Research in Science Teaching, 41(5)*, 513-536.

Shapin, S. (1996). *The Scientific Revolution*. Chicago: The University of Chicago Press.

Yager, S. O., Yager, R. E., & Lim, G. (1999). The Advantages of an STS Approach Over a Typical Textbook Dominated Approach in Middle School Science. *School Science and Mathematics, 106(5)*, 248-260.

Zeidler, D. L., Walker, K. A., Ackett, W. A., & Simmons, M. L. (2002). Tangled up in views: Beliefs in the nature of science and responses to socioscientific dilemmas. *Science Education, 86(3)*, 343– 367.

Zeitler, W. R., & Barufaldi, J. P. (1988). *Elementary school: A Perspective for teachers*, New York: Longman.

INDEX

A

academic achievement(s), ix, xii, 120, 122, 126, 132, 133, 134, 135, 136, 138, 139, 143, 144, 145, 147

achievement, vii, xii, 21, 31, 44, 46, 47, 50, 59, 67, 68, 119, 120, 123, 124, 125, 126, 133, 135, 136, 139, 147, 148, 150, 152, 153, 154, 155, 156, 158

attitude towards science, 44, 123, 134, 138, 142, 146, 147

attitude(s), vii, viii, ix, x, xi, 3, 6, 24, 26, 27, 28, 29, 35, 38, 40, 43, 44, 45, 46, 47, 50, 52, 53, 54, 55, 56, 57, 59, 60, 61, 62, 63, 64, 65, 66, 67, 68, 71, 75, 81, 85, 99, 111, 113, 119, 120, 123, 125, 126, 127, 133, 134, 138, 142, 144, 146, 147, 148, 149, 150, 151, 152, 155, 156, 157, 158, 160, 161, 162, 168, 169, 170, 171, 174, 175, 176, 180

attitudes towards science, 44, 45, 47, 50, 124, 126, 134, 138, 142, 144, 146, 147, 169

C

classroom environment, xi, 28, 48, 50, 51, 57, 58, 59, 60, 61, 62, 67, 122, 140, 149

competence for learning, 132, 133, 134, 135, 136, 138, 141, 144, 145

competences for learning science, 124, 134, 137, 142, 143

constructivist approach, xii, 120

constructivist practices, 121

D

Design, 9, 13, 18, 25, 26, 150

discovery learning, xii, 120, 125, 147, 149

discovery learning strategy, 120

discovery skills, 121

discovery-supported science learning, 139

E

engagement, xi, 2, 5, 22, 45, 46, 47, 53, 71, 72, 75, 109, 110, 169

170 *Index*

G

gifted education, 28, 29, 30, 32, 33, 57, 59, 61, 67, 68, 69
girls in science, 28, 29

I

inquiry-based learning, x, 1, 6, 8, 9, 20, 152, 153
integrated NOS flow map, 160

K

knowledge, ix, x, xiii, 1, 3, 4, 5, 6, 8, 9, 12, 14, 15, 18, 20, 35, 38, 39, 43, 44, 62, 73, 77, 78, 79, 80, 83, 84, 85, 86, 89, 92, 94, 99, 100, 101, 106, 107, 108, 110, 113, 121, 127, 129, 137, 139, 149, 151, 153, 160, 161, 162, 163, 165, 166, 167, 168, 169, 170,171, 172, 173, 174, 175, 176, 177, 178, 181
Knowledge about the topic, 9

L

learning box(es), ix, xii, 120, 123, 125, 127, 128, 129, 130, 131, 136, 137, 138, 140, 141, 142, 145, 146, 147
learning by discovery, 139, 143
learning competence, 120, 123, 134, 137, 144, 146
learning environment(s), ix, x, 27, 28, 29, 38, 40, 48, 49, 50, 52, 54, 55, 56, 57, 58, 60, 61, 62, 64, 65, 66, 67, 68, 117, 121, 135, 140, 147
learning process, xii, 120, 134, 136, 137, 139, 146
learning science, 2, 42, 43, 121, 127, 132, 133, 141, 149

learning through discovery, xii, 119, 121, 136, 137, 138, 139, 141, 142, 145, 146, 147
learning through the discovery, 122, 136, 139, 141

N

nature of science, x, xiii, 104, 160, 162, 163, 164, 171, 177, 178, 179, 180, 181, 182

P

partnership, ix, xi, 2, 25, 72, 74, 76, 80, 81, 82, 83, 84, 85, 87, 92, 93, 94, 95, 96, 97, 98, 99, 100, 101, 102, 103, 104, 105, 107, 109, 110, 111, 114, 115, 179
perception, vii, 57, 71, 72, 80, 112, 175, 176

R

real-world problem solving, 9

S

science, v, vi, vii, viii, ix, x, xi, xii, 2, 3, 4, 6, 7, 9, 15, 20, 21, 22, 23, 24, 25, 26, 27, 28, 29, 32, 35, 37, 38, 39, 40, 42, 43, 44, 45, 46, 47, 48, 49, 50, 52, 53, 54, 55, 56, 57, 58, 59, 60, 61, 62, 63, 64, 65, 66, 67, 68, 71, 72, 73, 74, 76, 77, 78, 79, 80, 81, 82, 83, 84, 86, 88, 89, 90, 92, 94, 97, 99, 100, 101, 104, 105, 107, 108, 109, 110, 111, 112, 113, 114, 115, 117, 119, 120, 121, 124, 125, 126, 127, 128, 129, 132, 133, 134, 135, 136, 138, 139, 141, 142, 144, 145, 146, 147, 148, 149, 150, 151, 152, 153, 154, 155, 156, 157, 158, 159, 160, 161, 162, 163, 164, 165, 166, 167,

168, 169, 170, 171, 172, 173, 174, 175, 176, 177, 178, 179, 180, 181, 182

science achievement, 47, 62, 123, 124, 134, 136, 139, 145, 147

science attitude(s), 40, 45, 63, 124, 132, 133, 134, 135, 142, 144, 145, 153

science competences, 141

science education, x, xiii, 2, 27, 28, 39, 45, 59, 60, 61, 76, 81, 123, 140, 143, 151, 152, 154, 156, 160, 169, 170, 171, 177, 179, 181

science learning competences, 123, 126, 134, 137, 141, 144, 146

science learning skill(s), 141, 147

science teaching, xii, 115, 120, 123, 128, 136, 138, 140, 142, 180

scientific literacy, 2, 160, 163, 168, 171, 174, 176, 178

scientific process skills, 121

scientists, vii, xi, 45, 71, 72, 73, 74, 75, 76, 77, 78, 79, 80, 81, 82, 83, 85, 87, 88, 89, 90, 92, 93, 94, 95, 96, 97, 98, 99, 100, 101, 102, 103, 104, 105, 106, 107, 108, 109, 110, 111, 112, 113, 114, 115, 116, 163, 166, 172, 174, 179

secondary education, 28, 149

Singapore, vii, x, 27, 28, 29, 33, 34, 35, 36, 37, 38, 39, 40, 41, 45, 48, 56, 57, 63, 64, 65, 66, 67

skill(s), 2, 4, 5, 6, 21, 25, 29, 34, 35, 38, 39, 48, 81, 85, 99, 100, 107, 108, 122, 137, 141, 143, 147, 148, 152, 155, 160, 162, 168, 169, 170, 171, 174, 175, 176

STEM integration, 2, 3, 5, 20

stereotype, 72, 81, 96, 105, 109, 111

student achievement, 140, 145, 155

T

teaching through discovery, 125

technology-based teaching, 28